MAKE IT
Magnificent

By the same author

Overcoming Barriers to Learning: How a culture of care in schools
   helps troubled pupils learn

MAKE IT Magnificent

How to live your life to the full, love yourself and achieve your dreams

SHEILA MULVENNEY

ATTUNED EDUCATION

Make It Magnificent

First published in the United Kingdom in 2019
by Attuned Education
www.attunededucation.com

ISBN 978-0-9934761-2-9

Earlier versions of some material have previously been published on
the author's business websites www.attunedsuccess.com and
www.attunededucation.com, and in *Affinity Magazine*. Material that
previously appeared in *Affinity Magazine* is reproduced with the kind
permission of the magazine editor, Jane Fry. For more information
about *Affinity Magazine* visit www.affinitymag.co.uk.

Author photograph by Catherine Berry

Cover design by Colourburst Lithographic Ltd

For Dave, Rob, Charlotte, Joe and Josh,
who keep on making my life magnificent!
Thank You.

.

Acknowledgements

With grateful thanks to Lewis Williams of Cavalcade Books, who pulled out the stops to get this edited and ready for publication in record time and coped with my, at times irritating I am sure, optimism that it could be done.

Thanks to Catherine Berry for photographs taken without too much pain!

Thanks also to the many people I have had the privilege to encounter who have all taught me a little about life and how to love it!

It is probably no coincidence that this book is finally published following a few years where life has delivered a wide variety of challenges but also the friends and family to offer kindness, compassion and whatever else is needed to not only keep going but to keep on loving life!

Contents

Contents

INTRODUCTION
Are you ready?

"You are not stuck where you are unless you decide to be."
Dr Wayne Dyer

You only live once

In my life and work I come across a lot of people who are dissatisfied and frustrated with different aspects of their lives. In many cases they are simply not living the lives they want to live.

That seems very sad. After all, we only get one shot at life, and none of us know how long our lives will be, so it seems important to me that as far as possible we should aim to live life to the full and enjoy as much of it as we can. In short, we should do what we can to make our lives magnificent.

The purpose of this book is to help people do that, but first let's address some of the things you might be thinking right now!

What about life's challenges?

Life presents us with challenges. This happens to every single one of us. For some of us those challenges may be long-lasting and extreme, for others less so, but all of us will face challenges – I think we'd all agree that is a certainty.

But we can probably all also acknowledge that there are some people who face extreme challenges yet still manage to live a life that is fulfilling, successful and happy. Then there are those for whom life seems derailed by the smallest of hardships. The fact is that how we respond to these challenges has an important bearing on their impact upon our lives.

The fact is that life isn't fair, and some people face horrendous situations. There will always be aspects of our lives that are beyond our control, and I am in no way minimising the extreme challenges to health and wellbeing, personal safety, economic wellbeing and family background (to mention just a few areas) that many people face.

While we may be able to take a few 'protective steps', wars and natural disasters will keep happening for the foreseeable future. Poverty or economic insecurity will probably remain a feature of the lives of many people. Illness and disability will continue to affect humans. There will also be people who through malice or their own need hurt others. There will always be people who find themselves in the wrong place at the wrong time. In some ways we are all victims to the vagaries of life.

Sadly, this book will not put an end to the problems that life brings, BUT it will help you to take a look at your own life, identify what happy and successful mean for you and examine the changes that you could make and the steps you are able to take to make your life MAGNIFICENT.

What about me?

Humans are the same but different. There are many factors of happiness that all humans share. We all function best when we have our physical needs met to a comfortable level, but what 'comfortable' means will vary between people. Humans are social beings, and most of us function best when we have people we care about around us and when we feel loved and cared for by others, but within that as individuals we are different – for example, some need a lot more time alone and fewer friends than others.

We could therefore agree that most people want to be happy but what happiness means precisely will vary from person to person.

Similarly, with success – a term used a lot these days. As humans we often feel happier when we enjoy a level of success or satisfaction, but what that 'looks like' will vary from person to person.

This book is all about YOU. In its first part you will begin to identify how YOU define 'happy' and 'successful' as applied to your own life in the present time, before looking later in the book at ways YOU may be able to change to get more of the happiness and success that YOU want.

It's up to you

As with any article, book, workshop or course, what you get out of it will be determined in part by the commitment you make and the action you take. This book will present you with a number of things to think about, activities to do and some changes you may want to make. Whether or not you 'engage' with that process is up to you. As with many areas of life, we can exercise choice.

Reading the book but not engaging with the process will still be helpful for many people, BUT if you really want to see changes and to make your life magnificent, then you will need to decide to engage with the book not just read it. For some people now will be just the right time and for others maybe not – that is a decision for each individual reader. But remember that the fact that you bought the book means that at least some part of you is open to change and wanting to make life magnificent in some way.

You are not alone

I run a dedicated Facebook group for readers of this book, so as you work through it you can ask questions, make comments and share your journey with others on a similar pathway. The link to the group is below, and I look forward to welcoming you. But of course, this too is your choice and I know it won't be for everyone, so there is no pressure – this book is designed as a tool for you to use in the way that benefits you the most.

https://www.facebook.com/groups/makeitmagnificent/

Making your life magnificent

I chose the word 'magnificent' because for me it conjures up a feeling of something abundant and we live in a world that is abundant – that abundance may not always be shared evenly, but the natural world is abundant. So, let me ask, are you ready? Are you ready to make your life magnificent?

- Do you want to live a life where you experience as much happiness and fulfilment as possible?

- Are there areas of your life where you know you could be happier?

- Do you sometimes wish you could change parts of your life, such as work, relationships or responsibilities, or how you feel?

- Do you often feel unfulfilled or frustrated in one or more areas of your life? Well, now could just be the time to change that and start living a life that is your own kind of MAGNIFICENT.

Magnificent (as defined by Merriam-Webster)

"1. *great in deed or exalted in place …*

2. *marked by stately grandeur and lavishness*

3. *sumptuous in structure and adornment*

4. *impressive to the mind or spirit: sublime*

5. *exceptionally fine*"

Synonyms for magnificent (from thesaurus.com)

"*wonderful, glorious, brilliant, elegant, excellent, glittering, gorgeous, grand, grandiose, imposing, impressive, lavish, lofty, noble, opulent, outstanding, palatial, splendid, stately, striking, sublime, sumptuous, superb, towering.*"

PART 1
Right here, right now

CHAPTER 1
Life audit – What is good and what would you like to change?

"It doesn't matter where you are coming from – all that matters is where you are going."
Brian Tracy

Life audit

Congratulations, you've decided to take the first step.

We will start by taking a look at where you find yourself in your life right now, what's good and what would you like to change. But before we get going on that, I'd like to just say a word about the past as that often gets brought up at this point.

Putting the past in perspective

The past is the past. We live in a world with a time frame. Quite simply, the past is gone so we can't change it however much we may want to, yet for so many people the past still exerts a major influence on the present.

In some ways we can divide the impact of the past into two parts – things that have happened to us and things that we have done, though of course some events may contain elements of both.

Things that happen to us have an impact upon us, and some people understandably struggle with past events like previous traumas which can cause significant emotional issues. Some people manage to overcome these and find healing without specific therapy, but others find therapy may help.

If you find the past impacts your life to such an extent that it stops you moving forward or if your way of coping with the past has been to self-harm in some way to manage the emotions, through abusing drugs or alcohol for example, then it may be that some therapeutic input will help.

But for many others the influence is exerted via beliefs and mindsets, which of course do have an impact on our lives in the present. We will unpack this further in the next chapter, but what I want to think about here are the emotions of regret and guilt that are often associated with the past and particular choices we've made which might have hurt others or had negative consequences on our current life.

The first point to note is that *feeling emotions – feeling regret or guilt – cannot change the past.*

Maybe you have beaten yourself up for years about the past – chances are it won't have helped at all. You can't change the past, but you can change the way you frame it and the extent to which you let it define your life in the present and influence what you do now. So, if you were speeding as you drove and were caught, you may have been fined – that is a consequence of your actions. Some consequences of actions may be much greater, but there is often not a lot we can do about them, and this may impact where you find yourself today. No amount of giving yourself a hard time over it will change the consequence. Feeling guilty won't help, neither will regretting it.

In more complex situations where perhaps someone was hurt as a result of your actions then sometimes it may be appropriate for you to take the decision to make some kind of reparation. Sometimes it may be possible and appropriate to explain what happened or why you acted the way you did – but only if that won't further hurt the person concerned.

"We all make mistakes, have struggles and even regret things in our past. But you are not your mistakes, you are not your struggles and you are here now with the power to shape your day and your future."
Steve Marboli

The important truth is that the past cannot be changed, events cannot be made to unhappen and actions – those of any significance – cannot typically be easily undone. Certain consequences may just have to be dealt with, and however much energy and time you spend feeling regret or guilt it is not likely it will change things.

You can, however, change the way you view or frame those things and importantly you may be able to learn from them.

"You can't go back and change the beginning, but you can start now and change the ending."
C. S. Lewis

Starting now

Back to the present!

Let us start taking a look at our lives. It is often helpful to think of the different spheres in our lives; most people would think of some or all of the following:

- Health, wellbeing and basic needs

- Relationships with others – family, friends, work colleagues, neighbours etc.

- Relationship with self – how we see ourselves and our sense of esteem or value

- Work – this may be a job, your own business or study

- Home – literally where we live, both the actual dwelling and the area/town/country

- Fun – activities, hobbies, travel, exercise

- Finances – income, day to day finances and our sense of financial security

- Creativity – this may overlap with your work, say if you run a creative business, or your hobbies or study

There are of course overlaps between these different spheres and in some ways there are elements of hierarchy – if we have no secure place to live, we are unlikely to be worried about a holiday.

Activity 1

With this activity, as with others that will follow, I'm going to ask you to write some things down. You can do this on separate pieces of paper or you may wish to get yourself a notebook to use from now on as you work your way through the book.

So, grab your notebook or several sheets of paper. Write each of the headings on a separate page or sheet of paper (in the middle if you like spider type diagrams and at the top if you like lists) and then start writing what you see as the positives in that area and what are the negatives. You can use as many pages or sheets of paper as you like. I've given a few examples below to help get you started.

Relationships – family

Partner

Still in love, enjoy it when we have time together.

Wish we could have more time together, but work takes up so much time.

Children

Child 1

Feel very happy with his progress and our relationship.

Child 2

Love him, but lately all he wants to do is spend time in his room or argue.

Child 3

Love her, but she just challenges everything I say and sometimes I feel relieved when she says she'll be out! I worry that we'll drift apart.

Work

I never dread going to work, but the travel means long days.

I don't hate what I do, but I don't love it either.

I don't think I'm paid enough for what I do.

Fun

I love my weekly badminton, but I know it's not enough exercise really – I'd love to join a gym but can't afford it and haven't really got the time.

Glad we've booked next year's holiday – looking forward to it, but I'll have to save hard to get the spending money together.

Of course, these are just examples and yours will be very different, I'm sure. In order to get the most out of this activity I suggest allowing yourself some time to do it and then putting your notebook or sheets of paper away for a few days before looking at them again. We will talk about the role and power of the subconscious more fully in Chapter 7 later, but once you start to think about areas of your life the subconscious has a way of bringing things to the surface. Someone might write under the heading of 'work' that it is okay, but then a few days later return and acknowledge that actually they have never really liked it, they don't get on with colleagues, find their boss difficult and have no confidence in the product or service offered.

We can find ourselves having slipped into ways of not being very honest with ourselves, and so when we start to allow ourselves to examine our lives with honesty it might take a while to get to what we really think. Thankfully our subconscious will usually help us out, so once you have completed your sheets of paper pay attention to the thoughts you have about the different areas of life and what you have written, particularly those thoughts that seem to just pop into your mind.

When you have returned to it at least once then rank the different pages in order according to how happy/successful you feel that each area of your life is. While it is perfectly possible to be unhappy with every area of your life, many people find there are one or two areas that give the greatest cause for concern and if these changed, even a little, there would be a positive knock-on effect to other areas.

Highlight the themes

When you have ranked the different areas the next step is to notice any themes or patterns. For example, is money apparent in each area, or are relationships? They may be top of the pile, but it may also be that in the work area the biggest thing you'd like to change is relationships with colleagues. Perhaps the most noticeable thing is your relationship with yourself – maybe you lack confidence or feel that whatever you do you will never succeed and these thoughts impact almost every area of your life.

So, notice patterns and again keep an ear open for any promptings your subconscious may give you. The patterns that you spot at this stage may well be the mindsets we will see that you need to work on in the next chapter.

And be sure to keep what you have written. It's your life audit and I'll be asking you to return to it soon.

CHAPTER 2
Identifying your mindsets and limiting beliefs

"Once your mindset changes, everything on the outside will change along with it."
Steve Maraboli

At its simplest a 'mindset' is the name we give to a group of attitudes and beliefs a person holds. As humans we are faced with a huge amount of stimuli and information every single day, and we haven't always time to weigh everything we hear, see or come across. As a way of managing this wealth of information our brain develops schemas. We don't then have to make a decision each time we see a dog that it is in fact a dog and not some other furry creature with four legs, like a sheep or a goat. Our brain takes the information, and the schema we have means we will identify it easily as a dog ... unless there is something very unusual about it, in which case it may take our brain very slightly longer.

But we also have mindsets about concepts, systems, abilities, people and ourselves, and it is these that can cause problems for us. We have mindsets about all sorts of things, and they can be positive ones that help us or they can be negative ones. In the table below I have put some of the common mindsets that can have an impact on our success and happiness so you can have a concrete idea of what we are talking about.

Common mindsets and how they present themselves

Negative	Positive
Wealth	
I'll never have any money. I don't deserve money. People like me always struggle. I'm no good with money. Money is bad, dirty or dangerous. People with money aren't nice. Maybe I'd change if I had money. People might not like me.	It's okay for me to have money. The world is an abundant place. If I have money, I am not robbing others. I can use money to do good. I will still be ME with money. I will still have friends.
Success	
Things never work out for me. I always mess things up. I always give up too soon. Success always happens to others. I never have any luck. People might not like me if I am successful.	Sometimes things go wrong, but I can choose to carry on/try again. It's okay for me to be successful. Everyone gets some lucky breaks. How people respond to me is not my responsibility. If I am successful, I can help others.

Love	
I always knew I'd be alone. People like me don't find love. None of my relationships have ever worked. In the end I always ruin my relationships. It's not safe to love – I'll be rejected again.	I can be in a relationship if I want. I am a unique person. I could make someone very happy and I can be happy. It's safe to love. I am strong and I can cope with rejection if I have to.
Happiness	
I just never feel happy. Life is always just a struggle. Other people are always making me unhappy. How could anyone be happy with my life circumstances?	I can make a choice to be happy. I am responsible for my own happiness. Tough things happen, but I can choose how to react to them. It's okay for me to be happy.
Self-worth	
I'm useless at everything. It doesn't matter about me. What I feel doesn't matter. I have nothing to give. I always ruin things. I'm a bad influence.	I have strengths and skills. I have value as a person. My life and feelings matter. I can make a positive contribution. I am not responsible for everything that happens to others.

Activity 2

Now that we've seen what some common mindsets are and how they can impact both the way you might think and the way you might behave or act, it will be useful to think about the mindsets you currently hold.

For this activity we'll start with the mindsets in the table above as these are common ones that cause problems.

- Grab your notebook or paper and pen and write the word e.g. 'happiness' or 'success' in the middle of a new page.

- Look at the word and note down any thoughts you have about that word as you look at it – the kind of sentences in the table above but use your own. The more honest you can be the better.

- Then have another look at the sheets you wrote for Activity 1 and if any 'themes' emerged write down those words and repeat the exercise.

Where mindsets come from

People often ask this, so I'll answer this now, but the important point to grasp is that wherever they have come from and however they have developed you can change them.

Mindsets often begin to develop in childhood when our brains are like sponges, soaking up what people tell us or the attitudes we see displayed around us. If you grow up in a household where money is a problem and it causes stress and arguments, then as a child you may develop a view that money is something that causes problems. As you grow this view might be endorsed or modified by the experiences you personally have with money. All of this will shape your mindset.

Growth mindset and fixed mindset

The research and theories of psychologist Carol Dweck have shown that one of the key influences on our lives and therefore our success and achievements is what we believe about ourselves – very specifically, what we believe about our abilities and characteristics.

Through research and experiments, she identified two almost opposing mindsets which she called the fixed and growth mindset. They refer to the beliefs people hold about their own characteristics in respect of intelligence and learning.

The fixed mindset

This is characterised by a belief that who you are in terms of your ability, creativity and characteristics is fixed – set in stone, unchanging. The problem with this is that it can create a situation where criticism is seen as an attack on character, and if the underlying belief is that this can't be changed, then understandably this becomes personal and is to be avoided. If you believe that your abilities can't develop, then the temptation will be to stay well within your comfort zone for that area and avoid anything that challenges you, because the underlying belief is that the skill can't be improved.

The growth mindset

This mindset emphasises the fact that everyone can develop and that new skills can be learned, in essence that we are not ever 'finished works' but are always able to learn and develop ourselves in different areas. The thing that will bring about change is not just our aptitude but our effort and motivation, how we apply ourselves.

Of course, we need to remember that as humans we don't have a single view of ourselves; we may hold different views of our abilities in different areas of life. So, we might feel we are accomplished in one area but not in another. We may be more prepared to learn in one area than another.

The impact

But how can a simple mindset have such an impact on our lives? We have probably all heard that often learning takes place at the edge of our comfort zone, and in some ways there is always some stress involved in learning. If our belief is that there is always something new to learn, we are more likely to embrace learning. If there is something we can't do and we frame it as something we haven't learned to do 'yet', our response may be very different from that if we have the view that our abilities are fixed and we'll never be able to learn that skill.

Becoming aware of our lack of knowledge or lack of skill in an area is okay if we believe we can develop but not if our view is that we will never be able to do it. I wonder how often you may have said, 'I could never …' or 'I'll never been able to …'!

With such a fixed growth mindset, criticism in those areas may be painful and the likelihood is we will avoid putting ourselves in positions where we have to do those things.

The power of the growth mindset

By developing a growth mindset and encouraging children to develop a growth mindset we open ourselves and them up to the idea that we continue to learn and develop and that means it is safe to take risks, to stray out of our comfort zones. A growth mindset improves motivation and learning.

When working with children, or as a parent, it's important to encourage them, but this should be done in ways that encourage them to keep on learning – using phrases like, 'Don't worry if you can't do it **yet**.' Encourage them too with the fact that if they find something a bit hard that is a sign that their brain is growing!

Our response

One of the key things that mindset determines is how we respond to situations. When faced with something challenging are we likely to steer clear or, armed with a growth mindset, are we likely to respond positively to the challenge and put ourselves into position where we can grow and develop?

In the next chapter we'll look at how to change our thoughts, but for now let's take a closer look at limiting beliefs.

Limiting beliefs

A belief is something we hold to be true. You and I will probably share a huge number of beliefs between us, that earth is spherical, that the law of gravity exists, that people are all different, that what we do can have an impact on our health and so on. But we may also hold some different beliefs, for example about what happens after we die, the extent to which we should worry about global-warming, whether drugs should be legalised, or whether the death penalty should be brought back. Beliefs often develop in a similar way to mindsets (clearly they are similar concepts) and can be as deeply entrenched, but most of us will be able to call to mind times when a belief we held was, perhaps successfully, challenged. Someone who grew up in a religious home may, for example, come to revisit the beliefs they hold about other religions as they become adult and gain more experience of the world and others practising those religions. So, just like mindsets, beliefs, even the ones that may have been limiting you for years, can change.

"If you accept a limiting belief, then it will become a truth for you."
Louise Hay

Identifying beliefs that limit you

We often feel uncomfortable in areas where limiting beliefs operate and stop us doing things, so thinking about things you struggle with can often give you an idea of where to 'explore'.

Activity 3

Think about areas of life that represent a struggle for you.

It might help to look back to the pages you created for Activity 1 in your life audit.

This time look at the areas you were most unhappy in – the ones you wanted to see the greatest change in.

The chances are there will be some limiting beliefs involved there, so have a go at identifying what they are.

Limiting beliefs are often concerned with how you see yourself and your abilities.

If you're finding it tough to identify them, then think of a situation you'd find a bit difficult, perhaps meeting new people, and 'tune in' to the whispers you'd hear in your brain – probably negative self-talk like:

'You've got nothing to offer.'

'Who would want to talk to you?'

'You always mess it up.'

'You are sure to say the wrong thing.'

If that is what your subconscious is whispering, then it's safe to say there are some beliefs about YOU that are limiting what you can achieve.

Don't worry if you find it tough to identify them. As you go through the book you can come back to this exercise again and more importantly to the next chapter which covers what to do about them any time you suspect there is a limiting belief at work in your life.

What's next?

In the next chapter we are going to look at thoughts and how these can be 'managed' to help rid you of unhelpful mindsets and limiting beliefs, and more generally be used as a force for progress and productivity.

"Our limitations and success will be based, most often, on our own expectations for ourselves. What the mind dwells upon, the body acts upon."
Denis Waitley

CHAPTER 3
Managing your thought life

"You must learn a new way to think before you can master a new way to be."
Marianne Williamson

The power of thoughts

Thinking really is the beginning of everything. Any invention, accomplishment or activity begins with a thought. Surely that should give us the message that thoughts are powerful. And they are! In self-help and empowerment circles there is so much being written about the power of thoughts in shaping our lives in very real and tangible ways. Often, we see thoughts as something completely internal, which of course they are, BUT they have the power to create and shape things in the very physical realm in which we live.

It's sometimes easier to see how powerful thoughts can be when we think of negative thoughts. Imagine that you are afraid of something and then you must face it. Perhaps it's flying, an animal or water, for example. The thought itself, 'the fear', can actually be powerful enough to make you feel very real physical symptoms. So, someone who is afraid of flying might experience feelings of panic long before they actually get on the plane, and when they do get on the plane, even though everything is safe and going to plan, they may experience physical changes, such as a racing heart or difficulty breathing – symptoms typical of a panic attack.

Thoughts can cause physical changes!

Once we understand how powerful thoughts are, we can then realise that the same power can be used positively.

Attitudes

One of the other important things about thoughts is that they create our attitudes. An attitude in this sense is the position we hold with regard to a person or thing. So, if we *think* that flying is dangerous, our *attitude* will be that we don't want to fly.

This happens in all sorts of situations, of course, and our attitudes will also cause us to interpret things in particular ways which then strengthen our thoughts and attitudes further. If someone has low self-esteem, for example, they will be likely to lack confidence in their abilities, and if they apply for a job and aren't successful, they will be sure that it will have been because they are useless, NOT because there were hundreds of applicants for the job or that the employer wanted someone with more experience. On the other hand, a person who has high self-esteem and a generally positive attitude will, in the same situation, be more likely to think that it wasn't the right job for them after all, that the rejection was nothing personal and that something better will be just around the corner. How they frame the situation, the spin they put on it, is down to their attitude.

Similarly, think about meeting someone for the first time and imagine that you have heard they are a gossip, a bully and a fraud! What would your attitude be? Negative, I suspect, or guarded at the very least – and perhaps sensibly so. The way you think about them, in this case because of what you have heard, will create the attitude you have towards them. (This, of course, could change when you discover they aren't like that at all.)

Many of our attitudes are much more general: the way we think about the world, our jobs, success, money, relationships, the 'mindsets' and 'limiting beliefs' we spoke about in the last chapter – all of these stem from thoughts. Get the thoughts right, ensure they are positive, and our attitudes will be more positive, which in turn will 'attract' more positivity into our lives.

"Whether you think you can or think you can't, you're right!"
Henry Ford

Words

Like thoughts, words can be powerful. Obviously, what we say comes from our attitudes, which stem from our thoughts. So, take a minute and think about what you would say about important things in your life. Are your words positive and full of optimism or are they negative and always expecting the worst? They are a window on your inner thoughts and attitudes. So, if what is coming out of your mouth in your words is negative, the chances are your thoughts and attitudes are full of negativity too. And it's all your own work! The thoughts were yours and so was the attitude, but these can and need to be changed if you want a more positive fulfilling life.

Activity 4

This is best done over the course of a day, or even a few days.

Make a conscious effort to notice the things that you say. In particular, notice the negative things you say.

This can be tough because once we start thinking about what we say it may change.

Try simply to 'hear' yourself when you are in conversation with others, about anything.

Do you find yourself grumbling (about the weather, colleagues, work, life) criticising (others or yourself) or complaining (about anything)?

Make a note of the tendencies you notice.

Behaviour

Our thoughts, attitudes and words all have an impact on our behaviour, on the things we do, the way we act, and that in turn is what creates our world. So, if you think life is one long test of endurance, then your attitude will be negative, your words probably will be negative too and your behaviour will follow suit. You are creating, or at least perpetuating, a negative lifestyle. But it doesn't have to be this way; everyone has the power to change, and so often when I work with people they put a lot of effort into changing their behaviour (usually unsuccessfully) but no effort into changing their thoughts. Yet this is where behaviour begins.

"Change your thoughts and you change your world."
Norman Vincent Peale

It's easier to see how this works by using a negative example. Someone who has experienced rejection might come to think they are unlovable and that everyone will reject them sooner or later. Their attitude will be that people are not to be trusted because they will let them down and reject them. Their words will often be negative about either themselves or relationships, and they will behave in such a way as to make darned sure they are actually rejected. A whole negative cycle stems from their thoughts.

But this cycle can be changed and the place to start is by changing the thought patterns.

Reality check

I'm sure some people reading this will be thinking that I don't understand how difficult their life is. I get that – now isn't necessarily the best place to share my own story, but it is worth saying that almost everyone experiences some hardship. I know it is impossible to 'compare' experiences, but if you consider a few people who by anyone's standards haven't had it easy, you can find examples of those who somehow through and in adversity have managed to triumph. I am sure they have had dark days, times when it's been hard for them to keep going, but somehow they have.

Here's a few brief examples. I have just given one fact about the person (which of course doesn't describe a life but shows one aspect of the adversity they faced) and one quote.

Nelson Mandela - spent almost 30 years in prison on political charges.

"The greatest glory in living lies not in never falling, but in rising every time we fall." – Nelson Mandela

Katie Piper – was attacked with acid causing major damage to her face and eye (she has had 110 operations) and is now a television presenter and philanthropist.

"Your life is what you decide to make it." – Katie Piper

Stephen Hawking – a physicist and cosmologist who suffered from a rare form of motor neurone disease which gradually paralysed him.

"However difficult life may seem there is always something you can do and succeed at. It matters that you don't just give up." – Stephen Hawking

There are many more examples I could give – perhaps you are thinking of some or could look others up for yourself – people who have experienced great adversity but have still managed to live positive lives and inspire others. Life is full of adversity, BUT while we may not be able to control all that might happen to us, we can decide how we will respond.

Later, in Chapter 13, we'll look at ways to cope with disappointment, but it is important to acknowledge here that while we may need time to adjust, to grieve, to restore ourselves, there are many aspects of how we live our life that are up to us. The place where that starts is with our thoughts.

"Once you replace negative thoughts with positive ones, you'll start having positive results."
Willie Nelson

Taming those thoughts

As we go through our busy days it can be hard to give attention to our thoughts, but that doesn't stop them just appearing in our minds when we least expect it, or when we are trying to do things. The unhelpful ones have a way of crashing into our minds at very inconvenient times, when we are trying to concentrate on other things OR at night when we are maybe trying to sleep.

Of course, not all thoughts are negative, but the ones to be wary about usually are. They will often be reminders of things you've done wrong, things that didn't go well, mistakes you have made or judgements about your character – 'You are no good,' 'You always mess things up,' 'You are so lazy,' or any one of a hundred other negative thoughts about yourself and your abilities. In fact, this background thought 'chatter' has even been referred to as our inner critic, and like a wild animal it can tear through your mind and confidence demolishing everything in its wake. The other type of negative thoughts are worries, anticipating situations or possibilities that may never happen but nevertheless cause us considerable anxiety.

The good news is that you don't have to put up with it. In the next chapter we will look at some truths that are a good way of protecting yourself against the damage unruly thoughts can cause. But even before we come to those, you can start by following the steps below to 'tame' some of those thoughts.

1. Notice the thought

Our brains are immensely powerful, containing billions of cells, and it is estimated (by scientists at the University of Southern California) that in any day we will have 70,000 to 80,000 'thoughts' (https://www.reference.com/world-view/many-thoughts-per-minute-cb7fcf22ebbf8466).

My own view would be there are many more than that! But of course, many thoughts we don't give much attention to. We might think about things we are going to do next, notice things around us, or remember particular things in response to stimuli, but the kind of thoughts that are negative should be noticed. Any thought that 'judges' you or an aspect of your character needs noting, alongside any negative thoughts where the focus is on the 'downsides'.

2. Evaluate the thought

Obviously sometimes there are negative things in life, and simply pretending something is positive when it isn't is not going to help anyone to be happy, BUT if you find yourself always thinking about negative aspects of situations or of what could go wrong, then by challenging those thoughts you can feel a lot better. So, when you get those thoughts try to evaluate them: Is it true? Is it accurate? Is there another perspective I should be thinking about? We will look more at truths in the next chapter, and that will help, but for now when you evaluate the thought IF you decide it's not true or accurate, then replace it with another thought. Easier to write than to do, but it gets easier with practice. You have probably all heard about blue bananas? If I ask you not to think about blue bananas, the first thought that will come into your mind will be of blue bananas. So, getting rid of them usually means replacing them.

3. Replace it with a different thought

The way to get rid of a negative thought is usually to replace it with a more positive thought. If you are thinking about the things you didn't like about an event, for example, you could simply replace those thoughts with thoughts about what you did like about the event. If the thought relates to an aspect of another person, again think about a more positive aspect – they tend to be unreliable, BUT they are a good listener, or they are sensitive or any other positive point about them. Similarly, if it relates to an aspect of your own character – for example you might be telling yourself, 'You never see things through,' – then counter this either with examples – in this case, of when you have seen things through – or with another more positive character trait that you know you possess. If this doesn't work, then try to stop 'thinking' and concentrate on sensory input; notice what is around you how you are feeling in your body, essentially adopting a more mindful approach to being in the present (more on this to follow).

4. Repeat

It is very tough at first but with practice it gets easier. Remember also that occasional thoughts rarely cause problems; it is when they are habitual that negative thoughts can cause damage. Dwelling in negative thoughts will only ever lead to negativity, which is different from looking at some aspects of life that may be negative in some way.

"Being in the present moment is a major component of mental wellness."
Abraham Maslow

---

5. Build a different thought life

As I mentioned at the beginning of this section, usually we don't attend to all our thoughts as life is busy. (Although if we are doing repetitive tasks that don't take our full attention, we can find a lot of thoughts 'pop' into our mind.) But we can make a decision to have some time on a regular basis when we do attend to our thoughts. Or even better, try and have times when we are simply 'in' the present moment by practising mindfulness or meditation. That way we can get used to 'stilling' our mind and this can help. We can also be careful what we 'feed' our mind with and choose to concentrate on positive input. We can also make a conscious decision to limit the time we spend with people who are particularly negative. We will return to these ideas later in the book when we look at the habits you need for success and happiness.

For now, start to notice your thoughts and try to minimise the negative ones using the tips above. In the next chapter we are going to take a look at the truths you need to embed and acknowledge in order to improve your thought life and in turn your reality.

CHAPTER 4
The truth about you

In this chapter I'm going to introduce you to some truths. You can think of these truths as shields you can use when your mind fills with all sorts of lies. I know that might sound strange – that essentially you tell yourself lies – but the brain and specifically our subconscious is very good at wanting us to dwell on things that aren't true.

Having said that, our subconscious can be extremely useful and powerful, and we'll look at how that can help us later in the book. For now, let us remember that our brain receives a huge amount of input and generally wants to work for our good, but in essence some experiences may be 'reviewed' and consequences drawn from them that aren't particularly accurate. The subconscious takes in information like a sponge. So, as we saw in Chapter 2 when we were talking about mindsets, if you are called stupid or lazy by others, your brain can latch onto this and will store this information away for reference.

"The subconscious mind cannot tell the difference between what is real and what is imagined."
Bob Proctor

Also, if you have an experience where you have felt humiliated, perhaps a relationship ending badly or even a presentation or interview that didn't go well, the brain is always wanting to protect you so will draw from that experience to remind you that it didn't feel good. Then if these experiences are repeated, the 'lie' can start to feel like a truth. So, here are some truths about you that you can rely on and use when you need to in order to counter any of the negative thoughts that may become habitual. Remember YOU can control your thoughts; you can choose whether to attend to them or not, so having a truth to use instead is helpful.

You are of value

Every single human being has value. That is not about what we do or achieve but simply because we are human beings. It's a truth you need to let sink in a bit. If you are of value, that means you deserve to be treated with respect, dignity, kindness and compassion, just like every other human being.

"To the living we owe respect, but to the dead we owe only truth."
Voltaire

But what we learn as we go through life is that in order to be treated with respect, we need to respect others and we need to respect ourselves. If we can't accept our own value, how on earth can we expect others to see our value? Self-respect is vital for self-esteem, which is much more about how we see ourselves and evaluate our strengths than a core belief in our own inherent value. Without self-respect it is hard for us to take care of ourselves (why should we if we aren't that valuable?) and without self-respect it is easy to let others walk all over us and find ourselves in the role of victim. However, self-respect is not the same as ego, which is more about our importance rather than our value.

"You yourself, as much as anybody in the entire universe, deserve your love and affection."
Buddha

When we really start to believe in our own inherent value then validation from others becomes less important. This for some people can remove or lessen a fear of failure, which is often tied up with how others see or judge us. When we accept the truth of our own value then we compare ourselves to others less and the self-sabotage that can become a feature of many people's lives ceases.

Self-respect enables us to have relationships based on valuing rather than needing each other and enables us to take care of ourselves, as we can give ourselves permission to do things that we know are good for us rather than living a life where we try to keep everyone else happy, often riding roughshod over our own needs, assuming the needs of everyone else are more important.

You deserve to be happy, BUT it's your choice

Once you understand your own worth then it is easier to believe the truth that you deserve to be happy. We live only one life, and you are as deserving as anyone else of happiness. Look at babies and small children, providing they have their basic physical needs met and are given love and attention they are happy. They smile at other humans, laugh at things that amuse them. Happiness is a human emotion. Nothing more, nothing less, and to pretend that we can spend every moment happy is unrealistic. However, our happiness can increase when we make a choice that we want to be happy and start building a life that will make us happy. Happiness is not always about what happens to us but more about how we choose to respond and frame what happens to us. This doesn't mean we ignore other emotions; it's okay to acknowledge them, and it can be helpful to consider why they have arisen and what we can do to improve things, but wallowing in negative emotions OR situations won't help much either.

"The art of being happy lies in the power of extracting happiness from common things."
Henry Ward Beecher

If you can embrace the belief that you deserve to be happy, then there is no reason to put up with situations that make you unhappy if you can, in fact, change them. Even if there are things you cannot change, then you can still make a choice to find happiness where you can, even in the small things, and you can choose to make sure you build as many of those things as possible into your life.

"The key to being happy is knowing you have the power to choose what to accept and what to let go."
Dodinsky

But unless you believe that you deserve to be happy you are unlikely to make choices that allow you to be happy. The first step therefore might be convincing yourself that happiness is not just for others but it is something you deserve to experience as well.

Money is NOT Evil

Greed may have caused a lot of problems in the world, and the inequality in the way the world's wealth is shared out is at the extremes of poverty not something humanity should be proud of, but there can be nothing inherently evil about money; it is simply a system of exchange. Its only value is what a society places upon it.

"If money is your hope for independence you will never have it. The only real security that a man will have in this world is a reserve of knowledge, experience, and ability."
Henry Ford

The often-misquoted quote about money is that 'the **love** of money is the root of all evil' (from the Bible 1 Timothy 6:10). Note it is talking about the love of money NOT money. Those are entirely different things. Moreover, we can sensibly value money without loving it to the point of losing perspective or becoming evil. After all, money means we can buy the things we want, live where we want, do what we want to do, or travel where we want to go. But most people would sacrifice money for other things, health for example. There is also plenty of evidence that money of itself does not make a person happier (though obviously you can be much more comfortable in misery with money than without). Money alone will not make for happiness, and we have probably all read or know about people who have lots of money and simply aren't happy.

But lots of people find it hard to even talk about money, or even admit that they think it is important and are motivated by it at least to a degree. It's almost an unwritten rule that alongside NOT talking about religion or politics we don't talk about how much we earn. Money, if not necessarily evil, is certainly seen as something that is a bit dirty or vulgar.

The truth is there is nothing evil about money, even though some people may have used money in evil ways and some people may have done evil things to get money. That doesn't mean money itself is evil.

The reason our attitude to money is important, like our attitudes to happiness and success are, is that if we think it is something evil then why would we want it? If we think of money as something that harms lives or changes us in negative ways, then subconsciously we will make sure we never have it. We will limit what we earn or make, and if we do end up with money, we will make sure we get rid of it, perhaps in ways that aren't too sensible or beneficial.

"Money is a terrible master but an excellent servant."
P. T. Barnum

It's important to have a balanced view – money is certainly not the be all and end all of life, but it is okay to have money, to

THE TRUTH ABOUT YOU

earn it, inherit it, win it or make it (though for me there is also a rider that making money should be ethical and not exploitative of others). Money enables people to help others and do good.

Once we let that truth sink in then we open ourselves up to attracting more money into our lives, rather than assuming that whilst others may have lots of money, somehow that doesn't happen to folk like us, or that it is evil stuff anyway.

It's okay to be successful

People define success in all sorts of ways. Some people reading this may link it to wealth; others may link it to status or notoriety, academic or other achievement or personal success in terms of relationships. Whatever way in which you define it for yourself is fine. It is your life, and therefore its success must be on your terms. We often hear people talk of a fear of failure, which many people may experience, but a fear of success can be just as debilitating.

But why on earth would people fear success? Often because success means change; it might mean moving outside our comfort zone, doing things we haven't done before, or we might not be able to 'hide' in the same way. For others the fear may be that they themselves will change or people will view them differently – maybe they won't be so loveable, or maybe people will resent them.

"There are no limits to what you can accomplish, except the limits you place on your own thinking."
Brian Tracy

Again the causes may vary, but it will always be hard to keep moving forward if we are filled with fear. Subconsciously we may start sabotaging our own efforts, to protect us and keep us safe.

Sometimes the fear of success will only begin to manifest itself when you start moving forward and change begins to happen. Start to embed the truth that you deserve success, like everyone else, and that it is okay to be successful. Yes, it might bring change, but you will be able to manage that change. Also, when the other truths become embedded, that you are of value for example, then any fears that come from fear of the judgement of others will diminish; your value doesn't depend on what others think. Of course, it's possible your success may upset people, but that is okay too. While not setting out to upset people, it is also almost impossible not to at times. Other people's reactions are really not your responsibility.

Your past does not define you

Everyone's background is uniquely different, and whatever our experience of growing up was there will probably be some times when we were hurt. I have spent many years working with children in care and regularly train professionals on the impact of childhood trauma and adversity. Without going off on too much of a tangent, if there are issues with attachment or trauma in early childhood, then some parts of the brain simply may not be 'wired' the same way as others. (If you do want to read more about this, visit www.beaconhouse.org.uk.)

While it is true that in certain phases of life, during early childhood for example, rapid brain development occurs and therefore if the environment is not nurturing effectively some damage might occur, the good news is that, as modern neuroscience tells us, our brains retain plasticity. They keep the ability to reorganise pathways and create new connections. New experiences, learning and memory formation can all lead to changes. This means we can learn new ways to think and act, whatever our background or prior experience.

Of course, it is not a straightforward formula, and while genetic factors may influence our response to events and experience, our environment can play a big part as well. We learn from others around us and their responses to situations. People who have experienced trauma as a child or as an adult may find it tough to recover from and may need professional help. But within the context of how we see ourselves, the truth is we are not our past. Although the past may have had an impact on our current situation, we all can choose a different future.

"Your past is just a story and once you realize this it has no power over you."
Chuck Palahnuik

In addition to people who struggle with past experiences where they have been hurt, there are some people who find accepting what they themselves have done in the past is what stops them moving forward. The same truth applies; whatever the context for what we did, even if we regret it or regret the pain it caused others, we can move forward. Some consequences may have to be lived through, but everyone has the capacity to change. First, though, we need to accept the truth that the past need not define our present, or indeed our future.

"When you forgive, you in no way change the past – but you sure do change the future."
Bernard Meltzer

For some people being able to accept this as a truth may need a real thought shift, and some may struggle with either forgiving themselves for things they did or being able to manage the hurt others caused them. Some people may need professional help for them to do this. There is no shame in that. If the past feels like it is stopping you moving forward, then seek whatever help you need to be able to frame it in a way that doesn't keep causing you problems and robbing you of happiness now.

Activity 5

Reading is, of course, all very well, but real change will come once we allow these truths to really sink in with us.

Grab your notebook or paper and pen and write each of the truths down.

As you write each one, say it aloud to yourself – more than once.

Notice how you feel. Do you find an objection in your thoughts to it? For example, if you say, 'I am of value,' do you straightaway have thoughts come up telling you that you aren't really? If you do, then sit with those thoughts for a moment and see where they come from; do memories come to mind?

The likelihood is that some of the truths will be easier for you to accept than others, so work on the ones that you find to be a bit tough.

Some people have found it helpful to write the truths out on cards and pin them in places that they see daily as a reminder.

Don't underestimate the power of stating these truths aloud to yourself, every day if necessary, till they gradually sink into your thoughts.

Keep in mind that if you find one truth quite a challenge to accept, it may take a bit of work to get to that acceptance as the 'lies' in this area have probably been part of your programming for some time.

The fact that something is difficult or uncomfortable often means it will help us achieve a great step forward, so stick at it until you can feel a shift happening and can embrace all these important truths.

"In any given moment we have two options: to step forward into growth or to step back into safety."
Abraham Maslow

PART 2
Dreams and
destinations

CHAPTER 5
Big dreams

There are two main definitions of the word 'dream' according to the *Oxford English Dictionary*, the "thoughts, images, and sensations occurring in a person's mind during sleep" and "a cherished aspiration, ambition, or ideal".

It is dreams of the second kind we will be concerned with here.

We all have dreams, things we've always wanted to do, places we've wanted to go or people we'd like to meet. We also all have a sense of how we'd like life to be, and if we are adults, we probably also have a sense of whether our life is living up to the dreams we had or not. Even if we reach a position where we have achieved all we've ever wanted, then that may, in fact, cause problems for us because we should be motivated by our dreams and work to pursue them.

There is a sense in which dreams are perhaps thought of as being longer term and 'bigger' than specific goals. There is also, for many, a sense that the fact that they are calling it a dream implies it is something that will be impossible or unlikely for them to achieve.

Let us be very clear that needn't be the case. I acknowledge that if your dream was to visit the Moon and you are currently in your 80s, it's probably not going to happen, but, even then, there are companies offering civilian trips to the Moon in the next decade. The cost will be prohibitive for most, but this chapter is all about us not being defeatist, not limiting our dreams, and acknowledging that there are an awful lot of dreams that are actually achievable.

"Every great dream begins with a dreamer. Always remember you have within you the strength, the patience and the passion to reach for the stars to change the world."
Harriet Tubman

Incidentally, regarding the quote above, Harriet Tubman was an abolitionist and activist who was born into slavery then later escaped and rescued others from slavery. Dreaming big for her must have been a necessity.

Dreaming is important

We can probably all acknowledge that we tend to work harder and be more motivated when we know what it is that we want to achieve. I'm thinking longer term dreams here rather than short term goals. So, people may study for years to gain a degree or qualification, often spending a lot of money to do so or working jobs alongside study. The point is humans put the effort in because they first have the dream. It is the dream that motivates them. Think about people who have sailed around the world, climbed high mountains, run marathons, built their own houses, travelled to inaccessible places or risen to any one of thousands of other perhaps seemingly impossible challenges. They didn't just wake up one day and set off – they all had the dream first and that probably means they also all had doubts, but they let themselves dream big. The book *Four Mums in a Boat* tells the incredible story of how four ordinary working mums from Yorkshire somehow decided they needed a challenge and ended up rowing 3,000 miles across the Atlantic. Just imagine their thoughts and doubts, and on their first race they were disqualified for being unsafe, but they kept going and they achieved their dream. Now, their dream won't be for all of us, but the point is what we achieve is tied up with our dreams. If our dreams are small and we don't allow ourselves to dream big, then we are limiting ourselves.

"You have to dream before your dreams can come true."
A. P. J. Abdul Kalam

Children seem to have no problem dreaming, but as we grow, somehow we limit our dreams. Before we let ourselves dream we start telling ourselves that it's not likely or it will be too difficult or it won't happen to us. We go through a process, therefore, of filtering our dreams and limiting ourselves in the process before we even let ourselves have a BIG dream.

Of course, if we dream big, we open ourselves up to the possibility of failure, of not achieving what we hope. Yes, that is a possibility, but of course if we don't dream, we are unlikely to achieve those things either. That is why before we begin to dream, we need to make sure we have got rid of unhelpful mindsets and limiting beliefs and have embedded the truths that will make it possible for us to dream and to throw ourselves into pursuing those dreams.

Remember too that not everyone receives a round of applause and encouragement from everyone when and if they announce their dreams, quite the contrary; many people face negativity, doubt or even derision when they share their dreams. But while it may be uncomfortable and while listening to people whose opinion we value has a place, it is your dream and yours alone, so if you allow others to dampen or extinguish YOUR dreams you aren't really being true to yourself.

"The people who are crazy enough to think they can change the world are the ones who do."
Steve Jobs

Activity 6

Remember at the start of the book we completed a life audit?

Grab that now and take a few minutes to think about the dreams you have for the different spheres of your life.

As a minimum consider

- family/personal life

- work/business

- hobbies or creativity

but feel free to look at as many spheres as you like.

For each one think about a dream you have. Try to think big, but you may find it easier to put something 'medium sized' and then visit it again in a few hours' or days' time, and then GO BIG.

The aim of this is to come up with a few really big dreams

Sharing our dreams

Some people have dreams that they don't want to share and in many ways that is okay, but I will give a warning. There is nothing that makes a dream real quite like somehow putting it out there. If you find it hard to share your dreams, try asking yourself why. Is it because you are afraid of what others will say? Are you beset by self-doubt? Do you lack confidence in your own ability or perseverance to see it through? Whatever the reason, try to explore it a little and while it isn't important exactly when you share your dreams, or even who with, if they are to be fulfilled, then being open about them will be important at some stage. But first you must have a conviction about the dream in your own heart and mind. A friend once said to me that if you have a dream that you can forget about then it isn't really a dream. If you can let it go easily, then maybe it isn't really that important to you anyway, and unless you are completely convinced and committed to it then you will be unlikely to cope with the setbacks you are bound to experience along the way. Big dreams don't always come easy, so do dream big but make sure you own it in every part of you.

Overcoming obstacles

Having a dream is important, and believing in that dream and our ability to pursue it, even in the face of opposition (which may at times be well meaning), is also important. An awful lot of people who society would regard as great achievers have faced obstacles – think about J. K. Rowling's Harry Potter manuscripts being rejected or the fact that Steven Spielberg didn't get into the film school of his choice. In fact, even cursory research into the lives of people who have achieved great things will show that the pathway to achieving dreams is littered with obstacles. What often separates those who achieve their dreams and those who don't is their tenacity – their ability to get up and try again… and again… and again…

"Success consists of going from failure to failure without loss of enthusiasm."
Winston Churchill

Of course, this quote from Churchill doesn't mean that failure is to be seen as the end; in fact, it means the opposite. In almost everything there will be another chance, or a different way to get to the next step. But it is important to learn from what's happened – going blindly from one disaster to another without a bit of reflection would be crazy.

Obstacles will land in your path – that is pretty much guaranteed, and sometimes they may be so big that you can lose sight of what your dream was, another reason to make sure you have shared your dream. Some obstacles may mean you need to rethink your route, others may mean you need to revisit timescales and yet others simply need moving out of the way or getting over.

The type of obstacles you face will depend on your dream, but they may include opposition from others (even from those you love), practical difficulties, financial difficulties, personal health or fitness issues, and many other things besides, but almost every obstacle can be overcome in some way. See each one as an opportunity to take stock, review your journey and probably learn something along the way.

"Never give up on what you really want to do. The person with big dreams is more powerful than the one with all the facts."
Albert Einstein

Pursuing big dreams may mean some sacrifices, anything from getting up early to train, not spending as much time as you'd like with people you love or doing things you love. Counting the cost is important too, and sometimes people reframe things if the cost is simply too high. This is a matter of choice, but remember this is always *your* choice. Learning to listen to your heart and intuition is important as a 'check' on whether you are still on the right path for you. We'll talk more about intuition in Chapter 7.

Keeping your dreams alive

There will be times when you will feel incredibly motivated by your dream, when you feel like you are progressing well, and it is easy then to keep going. There will be other times, such as when you face those obstacles, when you will just want to forget about it all. Of course, that will always be an option but not one you should rush to take. There are always things you can do to keep your dream alive. After all, it is your dream, so at least part of you wanted it, so some part of it is probably worth keeping hold of whatever has happened.

You may have heard people talk about their 'why'. When we know why we want to do something then it is often easier to keep going.

Activity 7

Go back to the 'big' dreams you wrote down for Activity 6 and now for each one ask yourself why you want this.

Your 'why' will be individual to you, and yours to decide.

And sometimes there isn't really a why – and that's okay too. You're probably familiar with the reply first attributed to the mountain climber George Mallory in response to the question, "Why did you want to climb Everest?" and which has become a standard one amongst adventurers of all types asked to justify their objective, "Because it's there."

Although I think this quote from Edmund Hilary, who was the first climber to successfully reach the summit of Mount Everest, tells a different tale.

"It is not the mountain we conquer but ourselves."
Edmund Hilary

If you don't think you have a why, then ask yourself if you didn't pursue this dream how that would feel.

If you aren't bothered one way or the other, then it probably isn't really a dream you want to pursue.

Practical steps to keeping your dreams alive

- Break the big dream into steps. We find it easier to keep going when we track progress – in the next chapter we will talk about goals.

- Remind yourself regularly why you want this, or why you can't let it go.

- Don't let your dreams be swallowed up by the routine of life. Give yourself reminders – write them down and pin them on a notice board or put a post-it on a mirror or the fridge.

- Create a visual reminder like a vision board (we'll talk more about these later) and use visualisation (more to follow on this in Chapter 7).

- Talk to others who are encouraging about your dreams, and if others are involved schedule time for 'support'.

- Enthusiasm is sucked by negativity, so either limit time with those who are negative or don't talk about your dreams with them.

- Create a system of accountability – we'll look at this in more detail in the next chapter. Time slips by if we aren't careful, so accountability is very important.

- Think about a coach or mentor to support you if you haven't got a partner, friend, colleague or business partner who fulfils such a role. You will need both support and challenge; ensure that the person you choose can provide both.

- Take action – do things regularly that will move you forward.

- Be very specific about what you want to achieve.

Activity 8

The point of this activity is now to add some detail to your dream. This is an essential step before you can start setting goals.

Go back to the dreams you identified and pick one.

Write it out on a new page or separate piece of paper, BUT write it with detail. So, if one of your dreams is to have a bigger home for your family, then be specific about what kind of home you want – Do you want one extra room or three? A house with a garden or not? A house in a specific area or not?

Or if your dream is to start a business – What sort of business would it be? Would it be a physical business or online? Would you want to do it alone or as part of a team?

Or if your dream is to emigrate – Where to and when?

Or if your dream is to be happy in your personal life or in a fulfilling relationship – What would that look like for you?

I think you will be getting the idea.

Remember this is your dream but it's hard to achieve if you aren't sure what you want. Many people tell me when I ask them to do this exercise that they feel greedy for asking for so much, or that they don't want to give themselves something on paper that they might not achieve.

If those thoughts are still popping up, then remind yourself of the truths we considered in the last chapter and do a bit more work on challenging those limiting beliefs you might have.

If you are reading this book, then you are on a journey to creating a life that is magnificent. You are free to dream, and dreaming is one essential step in creating a life you love.

When you have done that, and you may need to revisit it a few times, then let's move on to the next chapter about goals and intentions.

CHAPTER 6
Goals and intentions

We ended the last chapter by thinking very specifically about our BIG dreams. So, the next step now is to start pursuing those dreams. But we all find manageable steps easier than just one huge task. Now that you have been specific about your dream you can think about what some of the logical steps to achieving what you have specified might be.

Let's take an example of wanting to start your own business.

Now that you have been specific about what that business may be and added some degree of detail to the picture then think about the first step. Maybe it would be market research around similar products, or maybe if it is a service-based industry it would involve you undertaking training or gaining a specific qualification that will enable you to offer that service. This sort of research and planning will take place long before you make decisions on the detail of the business name or where it will be based.

Look at the last thing you wrote about your dream and see if any steps are obvious to you. At this stage they can be large steps that may incorporate several others within them, but it is important to think in some degree of detail. Let's go back to the business example and say someone wants to be a diet coach or nutritional adviser. It may be they already have qualifications, but it may be they haven't. Remember dreams might mean stepping outside of what is or has been familiar to you. If the first step is to gain a qualification, then there needs to be a step where they need to do some research about available courses, and maybe then saving to afford the course, maybe even reducing hours at work or making some other adjustments to allow time for study. Such things will be important stages in moving towards your dreams, as are some specific goals and intentions.

Goals and intentions

There are clearly similarities between these, but I can't help seeing them as a bit different. To me an intention is something more specific than an overall dream but not as specific as a goal, which may be quite task oriented. If we stick with the example above, the following might be an example of the dream, an intention and a goal.

Dream – to have a diet/nutrition business

Intention – to help people regarding their nutrition by providing advice and guidance

Goal – to gain a specific qualification in nutrition

People will divide these differently and it really isn't worth getting hung up on the words, but let's continue to look at intentions and goals, and that means having a bit of a look at abundance and the law of attraction.

Abundance and the law of attraction

If the concept of attracting abundance is new to you, then I would recommend reading *The Secret* by Rhonda Byrne, but to explain the basic concept here: the notion is that the universe is abundant and that we can attract some of that abundance into our lives by being open to what the universe has to give us AND by letting go of some of the mindsets and subconscious beliefs that block the flow of abundance into our lives. We talked about those mindsets and limiting beliefs earlier in this book.

"See yourself living in abundance and you will attract it."
Rhonda Byrne

If you find the idea that the universe is abundant difficult to accept, then just look at nature: trees laden with blossom or fruit, gushing waterfalls and rolling mountain ranges. It is both abundant and awe inspiring. Generally speaking, we have little to do with that abundance – nature manages it all on its own. So, the first step to attracting abundance into your own life is believing that the universe is abundant.

We talk of the law of attraction, and while we don't usually have much trouble accepting the law of gravity – apples don't fall downwards from trees sometimes; they do it every time they fall because of the law of gravity – some people struggle with the notion of abundance attraction as a law. The law of attraction means that the universe will give us what we attract. How do we attract things? The answer is through our energy and 'vibration'. All of life is energy, and energy flows through our bodies constantly. Ever wondered why some people seem to have all the luck? – often it is because they are attracting that luck through their energy and thoughts.

"I attract to my life whatever I give my attention, energy and focus to, whether positive or negative."
Michael Losier

We've already talked a bit about obstacles and setbacks – life sometimes throws us lemons and that will remain true. BUT in the realm of personal endeavour and our response to those lemons then the law of attraction will come into play. In Part 3 of the book we will look at how to make things happen in practical steps and there'll be a bit more detail, but for now just keep in mind the powerful notion that our thoughts, and the emotions they generate, will play a part in what we 'attract'.

"Whatever you hold in your mind on a consistent basis is exactly what you will experience in your life."
Tony Robbins

Setting intentions

An intention is an explicit message to yourself and the universe that you want to see certain things happen. Think now about an intention you have. Be specific, and you might find it helps to write it down. With me there is usually an element of altruism in my intentions, so, for example, while I might want a bigger house, part of my intention would include a desire for my family members to have the extra space that would benefit them – not that there is anything wrong in wanting a bigger house for any reason, but most people have a personal 'why'. In my view intentions are shaped by our individual personality and perspective, our intrinsic values and beliefs. My intention might be to have a successful business but one that didn't exploit anyone and was ethically and morally 'sound'. It would be incompatible for me to have an intention that involved doing harm to another individual as that wouldn't reflect my core beliefs and values.

"Your intention rules your life and determines the outcome."
Oprah Winfrey

Intentions need to be authentic, and that fits with the notion of having the right 'energy' and therefore attracting the abundance we seek. After all, if we hope the 'universe', whatever that might mean to us as individuals, will help us manifest what we seek, then generally we'd want to be seeking things that heal rather than harm. Though I know opinions with regard to abundance and manifestation may vary a bit, I think the notion of Karma is relevant here. If we wish for harm to others, then it is likely to harm us.

Activity 9

This activity is about setting and announcing your intentions.

So, if you haven't already, now is the time to think about some 'intentions' in relation to your dream.

If you look on the internet, you will see a whole host of ways of setting intentions. Some recommend an intention setting ritual;

others feel it is best done in meditation. Setting an intention is planting a seed in our brains, which in turn makes us more receptive to certain prompts. If I set the intention that I want to have a different job, for example, the very fact that I have set the intention will make me more 'receptive' to any news about jobs. It awakens an aspect of our consciousness.

A key point is that you must announce the intention in some way to yourself and to the universe. Either say it aloud or write it down or do both. But do allow yourself a bit of time to do this; try writing down a few variations on the same theme then leave them for a few hours and come back to them to see which one resonates with you the most – maybe none will, in which case try it again. When you get an intention that feels right for you then say it aloud more than once and write it on something you can either have with you as a reminder or put somewhere you will see regularly. The key to this is to find ways to keep it alive for you – it's not that you need to recite it daily necessarily; it's about it sinking into your subconscious, and the way that happens differs from person to person.

*　*　*

Whole books have been written about abundance, intentions and affirmations, so I am not going to pretend I can cover everything in one short chapter, but affirming your intention is an important step – the reminding yourself of it, restating it, in a sense recommitting to it. But again, there are differences between intentions and affirmations; an intention is future based and an affirmation is rooted in the present, but they may refer to the same thing.

If we stick to the example above about the nutrition business, some intentions and affirmations could be:

Intentions

"My intention is to help people by offering advice and guidance about nutrition."

"My intention is to build a business where I help people achieve their nutrition goals."

Affirmations

"I am learning all I can about nutrition."

"I am open to finding the best ways to guide people on their eating habits."

Affirmations can be very helpful towards maintaining healthy mindsets, for example in reminding yourself of the truths we talked about in Chapter 4.

But any intention will also need action, and to do that in a planned way which doesn't overwhelm us often means identifying specific goals so that we can do things and take action.

"Take action! An inch of movement will bring you closer to your goals than a mile of intention."
Steve Maraboli

Goals

These are usually task based and generally should be SMART, Specific, Measurable, Achievable, Realistic and Time-limited. There is a school of thought, though, that says the A should stand for Aspirational rather than Achievable or Attainable – yes, goals must be realistic but if they are too easy, they may not move you forward very much.

Once again personality comes into it. Some people would feel overwhelmed at the start if a goal wasn't easily attainable. As in other areas, some people are comfortable with taking on a lot at the outset and others feel more comfortable working with one small step at a time, which they'll massively enjoy ticking off before moving on to the next one.

Personally, I love goal lists and mine are long and some individual goals are huge – which might not always be helpful, but over the years it seems to be how I work best. I do enjoy crossing things off, but I can certainly perform well working towards several goals at once.

The key here is simply trying different ways and finding what works for you, remembering that as we develop and grow we may need to change. Even if you think you have a way that works for you, don't be afraid to try new ways which might work even more effectively. (Yes, I have taken note of what I've written!)

Once you have an intention then your goals will be the tasks and steps you need to take – the actions to get you towards your stated intention and dreams. In the dream of the nutrition business where the intention had been around learning the goals would be fairly straightforward and could involve:

- Researching courses (both online and at local colleges)

- Deciding on the one you want to follow

- Enrolling or completing application forms

- Making arrangements to be able to attend (childcare or job discussions about time off etc.)

- Doing any pre-course planning/reading/preparation e.g. buying equipment

Each of these could be written as a SMART goal, and that spurs a lot of people to keep up the pace of action taking. Of course, this is obviously just one example, and the goals you set your self will vary. It's also worth remembering that you may be working on several things at once, so in this example it may also be that at the same time you're checking out other businesses offering the same or similar service and prices they charge, or thinking about where you will run the business, and so on.

Several intentions and goals can run concurrently and often need to if you are to keep moving forward with any kind of pace.

"Setting goals is the first step in turning the invisible into the visible."
Tony Robbins

Activity 10

So, now is a good time to get your notebook or some paper and jot down some goals related to your first intentions. Try to make sure they are SMART, and I'd aim for at least three, though you might have many more (as long as the length of the list doesn't itself become a demotivator). In terms of a timeframe, it really does depend on the goal. Taking the example above, if you need to find out about courses, then the goal might involve undertaking the online research within, say, the next 24 hours but allowing a greater period of time to plan, arrange and undertake a visit to the local colleges.

You'll find some tips for staying motivated later in the book, but for now set some goals giving some that you can achieve in the next day or so and some that you'll achieve in a week, and see how you go with those. Even if you don't achieve them within your timeframe, the fact that you have written them down means they are more likely to happen.

Remember this is all about you, your dreams, your goals and your life; it is unique to you, so it can be done your way – as always, the choices you make will be your own.

"Dream your own dreams, achieve your own goals. Your journey is your own and unique."
Roy T. Bennett

In the next chapter we are going to consider how we can use visualisation and the power of our subconscious to help us achieve our dreams.

CHAPTER 7
Visualisation and the power of your subconscious

"Whatever we plant in our subconscious mind and nourish with repetition and emotion will one day become a reality."
Earl Nightingale

Your subconscious

If you've read the book up to this point, then you will have an idea that the subconscious is powerful. You will be aware that it doesn't do well with negatives (don't think of blue bananas) and that, in the effort to manage the enormous amount of information that we get and experiences that we have, sometimes unhelpful subconscious beliefs and mindsets 'settle', but we can generally get rid of those by telling ourselves what we know to be true and rejecting those unhelpful beliefs that operate at a subconscious level.

We take in a lot of subconscious messages; that is how some advertising is so effective. Pick up any household brand item and you will probably know a jingle or tagline about it that you have never consciously learned but it's there, because you have 'picked up' the message at a subconscious level.

But it is also possible to harness the power of our subconscious for our own benefit, so let's look at some of the ways we can do that and begin by considering how we can tune in to our subconscious.

The nature of the subconscious is obviously that it operates under our consciousness. We are often not aware of it, but it can exert an influence on our thoughts, feelings and actions. It is easy for the subconscious 'voice' to be crowded out by the busyness and stimuli of each day. But we can learn to tune into it when we try to. There are particular times when it is easier to listen to that voice, times when other voices aren't so loud, when you are doing things that don't require a lot of conscious thought, certain household tasks, repetitive jobs, walking, or anything that doesn't take your full mental effort. At times like that just 'notice' the thoughts that arrive in your mind.

Similarly, the times when we are either just drifting to sleep or when we first wake can be when we get a window to our subconscious, so again just notice the thoughts you have then. As we go through our day we have an internal mental chatter, a kind of inner commentary, and this tends to come straight from our subconscious. Sometimes it is an 'inner critic', that voice that is always telling you negative things, and it is possible to silence that (more on this in Chapter 13) but for now let's just stick with tuning in.

Our subconscious voice might also be evident when we start to think about dreams, intentions and goals, so notice the thoughts that come up then. As we discussed earlier, these might reveal some false beliefs, but they might be thoughts that can point you in the right direction, give you ideas or help you think about things you may not have considered.

The first step in harnessing the power of your subconscious is to learn to listen. That means you will decide to tune in at the times mentioned above, but also sometimes it's helpful to set time aside when you will attempt to quieten your mind for the purpose of allowing the subconscious mind to have a voice. You may also want to make a note of the thoughts you have.

"The subjective mind is ... controlled by suggestion ... the subconscious mind accepts all suggestions; it does not argue with you, but it fulfills your wishes."
Dr Joseph Murphy

Relaxing can be hard for a lot of people, but there are techniques that you can follow if you find this difficult. Pick a quiet place and take a few deep breaths and try to focus on your breathing. Notice the feeling of the air entering your nose and filling your lungs and the feeling as you let it go. Listen to the sound of your breath. Thoughts will come into your mind, but what you are aiming for here is a time to 'still' your mind. So, as the thoughts come do just let them go one by one and bring your focus back to your breathing.

Some people practise mindfulness, meditation or yoga regularly and this can help to open up a channel to the subconscious. There are several guided meditations and scripts that can help, but if this is new to you, then start simply by making a time to be still part of your regular routine and you will probably notice it becomes much easier to 'hear' your subconscious.

Harnessing the power of our subconscious can also be useful as it helps us use our intuition to give us a bit of guidance along the way.

"Our subconscious minds have no sense of humour, play no jokes and cannot tell the difference between reality and an imagined image. What we continually think about eventually will manifest in our lives."
Robert Collier

Using our intuition

Many of us will have had the experience of having a feeling we should do something that we maybe hadn't planned, like taking a different route home, or calling a particular person, only to find later that there were road works on the usual road home or that there was an important reason why the person really needed that phone call. These are examples of using our intuition, acting not just on rational thought and reason but going with a gut feeling, even if we don't understand why.

TheFreeDictionary.com defines intuition as, "The faculty of knowing or understanding something without reasoning or proof, or an impression" or "insight gained by the use of this faculty".

Many of us see intuition as a hunch, that feeling we have, usually unbidden, about a particular situation or course of action that we sense we need to take. I'm sure you will have your own examples you can think of, but here are a couple of mine. When I went into labour with my second child my then husband was away and, it being the middle of the night, I was unsure that I'd be able to contact my 'reserve' person, but when I phoned her she said she'd been awake for ten minutes already and knew I would call. On another occasion, I remember looking at a house with a view to buying it and having a gut feeling that there was something not right about it, though on the surface it ticked all our boxes. A long time later I noticed it was still up for sale, and when I enquired I was told that it had a major subsidence problem, so while several people had started the process no one had actually bought it. Obviously, a survey would have revealed this, but we'd have wasted a lot of time and some money.

Are we all intuitive?

Many people believe that it is our ability to reason that makes us different from animals. They act on instinct, whereas we can be rational and logical – we can apply our powers of reason to our instincts. This is a good thing; we certainly wouldn't want to make every decision or act 100% of the time on instinct. But neither is it something we should block out entirely, or even think of as unscientific. Intuition comes from our subconscious and so will be driven by a lot of past experiences and previous learning. This may not always be helpful, but that doesn't mean it never is. The key for us is using it to help us, which means not forgetting logic and reason but not ignoring our intuition totally either.

Sometimes we are quite prepared to follow our intuition. If we are, say, walking alone and get a feeling we shouldn't walk up a particular street, many of us would follow our instinct. With buying houses, booking holidays and even going for new jobs you will often hear people say that something either 'didn't feel right' or that it 'just felt right' – there may be elements of logic and reason at work there, but there is also a strong sense of intuition or instinct.

In fact, the US military is actually investigating how they can train personnel to be more intuitive when making a decision or judgement, and the use of intuition in business and management is something that is becoming increasingly recognised as an important tool in the decision-making process.

"Insight is not a lightbulb that goes off inside our heads. It is a flickering candle that can easily be snuffed out."
Malcolm Gladwell

Intuition is something that we all have; it is indeed a sixth sense. But for many of us, having had years of telling ourselves, or others telling us, not to listen to that intuitive voice, it can take a bit of practice to 'hear' it again.

This is part of tuning into our subconscious, so finding times when we quieten our minds will help. Intuition is a whisper rather than a shout, and if our lives are busy and we constantly have phones, tablets, radios and TVs and people demanding our attention, it can be hard to hear.

Very often intuition is associated with creativity. Certainly, using the creative part of their brains seems to put people in greater touch with their intuition. Taking notice of things is a great way to improve your intuitive powers. Intuition comes from within but is often based on previous experiences or learning, and being observant seems to help the process.

But is it right to always trust your intuition? There are no clear-cut answers, but I find using what I call the 'peace' process helps me. If I think about following that course of action, how do I 'feel'? Do I feel peaceful about it or does it throw up a lot of anxiety? If it does make me anxious, that doesn't necessarily make it wrong – remember our brains are complex organs with billions of neurons, and as we go through life our brain makes all sorts of connections based on experiences, many of which we may have consciously forgotten – but I would certainly notice if it felt right, and for me that is associated with a sense of peace. It doesn't mean it will be easy and I may feel anxious about certain steps, but there will be a sense of peace about the course of action. I would acknowledge other feelings but be aware of my sense of peace.

If it was a significant decision, I would also talk to others about it, people I trust, people who know me well, and I would take their views into account. I would also give myself permission to change my mind. If I follow my instinct, then later get a feeling that it wasn't a good plan, I am free to change. Learning to follow our intuition and use it for our benefit takes time and practice, and while it might not be an exact science it is something we can learn to get better at.

"Intuition is always right in at least two important ways: 1. It is always in response to something. 2. It always has your best interest at heart."
Gavin de Becker

But in addition to learning to listen to our intuition we can also harness some of the power of our subconscious by using visualisation.

Learning to visualise

It seems as we grow up we get lots of exhortations not to daydream, which in many ways is what visualisation can be, but rather to focus and concentrate on the here and now. It's often regarded as a waste of time. In fact, the term 'dreamer' itself can be somewhat derogatory, implying that the person is not productive or even successful.

Yet increasingly evidence seems to suggest that not only is visualisation NOT a waste of time but it can help us in all sorts of ways.

We have said before that thoughts can be powerful, and one of the most effective ways of making them so is to use the tool of visualisation. It is used in a number of areas to improve performance in a variety of different ways. Many people may have heard about it in relation to sport, as nowadays a lot of sportsmen and women are open about the way they have been coached to use visualisation as a specific technique.

"Part of my preparation is I go and ask the kit man what colour top we're wearing – if it's red top, white shorts, white socks or black socks. Then I lie in bed the night before the game and visualise myself scoring goals or doing well."
Wayne Rooney

Depending on the particular sport, different visualisation techniques will be used to improve performance, whether that's scoring more goals, running more quickly, getting a longer drive in golf or a better backhand in tennis. Much time will be spent physically training but also visualising the improvements they want to see or the specific 'goal' they want to achieve.

"Often, I visualize a quicker runner, like almost a ghost runner, ahead of me with a quicker stride. It's really crazy. In races, this always happens to me. I see the vision of a runner ahead of me, maybe just 15, 20 meters ahead of me, and the cadence of that runner, which is actually me in the future, is a little quicker, so if I'm going (his rhythm/breathing), then my ghost runner, the vision of me, ahead of me, like opening up and just going for it, is quicker."

Gabe Jennings

Recent scientific advances have enabled us to see just why visualisation appears to be so powerful. According to Lynne McTaggart in her book *The Intention Experiment,* the brain does not appear to differentiate between the thought of an action and a real action. She reports on an experiment using EMG (electromyography) where it was discovered that when downhill skiers mentally rehearsed their runs the electrical impulses sent to the muscles were the same as when they physically engaged in the runs.

But it is not just in the field of sports that visualisation has proved effective. Various artists, including singers, writers, poets, actors, musicians and painters, have used visualisation techniques to improve their creativity.

"Everything you can imagine is real."

Pablo Picasso

More recently there has been an increased emphasis on the power of visualisation in both business and personal success – the idea being the same, identify what you want to achieve, what the goal is, what success looks like and then visualise it. It has also been used effectively in schools and universities as a tool to aid learning.

It is important to remember that visualisation can also be used to deal with negative thoughts. This is a technique that has been used with children, but it is just as powerful for adults to imagine they are ridding themselves of an unhelpful emotion.

"I have a system of ridding my mind of negative thoughts. I visualize myself writing them down on a piece of paper. Then I imagine myself crumpling up the paper, lighting it on fire, and burning it to a crisp."
Bruce Lee

Visualisation is more than daydreaming. It involves making a conscious decision about what you want to achieve, and you've done this when you thought about and wrote down your big dreams.

Activity 11

- Set aside a few minutes and sit quietly.

- Take a few deep breaths to quieten yourself.

- Remind yourself of your big dream.

- Add as much detail as you can to your picture of your dream; make it as detailed as possible.

- Visualise it and try to connect with the emotions you would feel.

Remember to visualise the outcome not the process. Think of scoring the goal, making more money and what that would mean for you in real life terms, landing the particular job that you have dreamed of, being that confident person that you would love to become, running that business you dream about, being happy in a relationship, or whatever your dream happens to be.

"Imagination is the highest kite that can fly."
Lauren Bacall

When you are thinking about it think in as much colour and detail as you can; think in pictures – remember your brain impulses will be reflecting what you are thinking about. Don't give up when nothing happens immediately; get used to just carrying on with those visualisations. What many people find is that visualising helps them take the right steps to get where they want to go. It would seem silly for a footballer to imagine scoring goals if he didn't bother even turning up to training. Visualisation is a technique and can be powerful, but it is not a magic wand. Many people find visualisation is most effective when coupled with meditation or mindfulness exercises, as we discussed above, but that is a personal choice.

Allow yourself to dream and imagine your success; the more you concentrate on those positive affirming thoughts the more likely it is that your life will begin to reflect that.

"It's a psychological law that whatever we desire to accomplish we must impress upon the subjective or subconscious mind."

Orlson Swett Marden

CHAPTER 8
Reflection and progress

Learning to reflect

While reflection is something we all do at times, it would probably help us all if we could learn to do it with greater frequency and more depth.

Not many of us, either male or female, would consider ourselves ready to leave the house without a check in the mirror, but we also probably all know some people who insist on checking their appearance not just several times in a day but every time they pass a vaguely reflective surface. Why do we do it? Well, usually we want to check that we look the way we want to, and looking in a mirror may cause us to put on more lipstick, straighten a tie, comb our hair, select an alternative piece of jewellery or a different jacket, or even go completely back to the drawing board and change our whole outfit. The process of considering ourselves in the reflection of a mirror is an important part of our finished product; we take some action, say, getting dressed or styling our hair, and the reflecting process – in this case looking at ourselves in the mirror – allows us to see if we achieved the results we intended.

But the type of reflection I want to consider now is not to do with appearance but rather other aspects of our lives. Remember one of the reasons we use a mirror is to check we got the desired results; well, the same is the case with other types of reflecting – are we heading where we wanted to go, living the life we planned, feeling the way we want to about ourselves and our relationships, or is life just drifting by? The process of reflecting can help us take stock and, if necessary, change direction. This is an especially important process once we have started to actively move towards certain dreams and goals, or indeed to change any aspect of our lives.

"Reflection is one of the most underused yet powerful tools for success."
Richard Carlson

When is a good time for reflection?

The straightforward answer is any time and all the time. In many ways, the more we do it the better, while stopping short of obsession. There are, however, some key times that seem to be made for reflection, times like birthdays, anniversaries or New Year. These are good times to think back over the last year, or decade, and in particular the resolutions people make at New Year will often follow some reflection – I don't like my size/shape, so I'll resolve to diet, or I'll exercise more etc. You might ask yourself if you're happy with your job or your relationship, or whether you're where you thought you'd be at this stage in your life. If you're not, you should ask yourself if you're happy with where you find yourself or whether you really need to make some adjustments in order not to feel regret further down the line. Hopefully this is a process you began in Chapter 1 with your life audit.

Another key time for reflection, and one that others can help us with, is following significant life changes: moving to a new house, getting a new job, starting a new relationship, becoming a parent, starting a course or setting up your own business. At such times friends and family will often ask, *How's the new... house/job/course?* or whatever it happens to be. In the same way that seeing our reflection in a mirror may make us make a few changes, so too can answering these questions. Of course, we may not reveal the whole answer to whoever asked the question, but just being asked the question will cause us to reflect and consider how things are, however briefly. The job may be good but the hours too long, or the house may be further from friends than you'd considered, or the course not as interesting as you'd hoped.

While it may happen quickly, the process is important in determining for yourself how you feel about these changes. If everything is perfect or at least pretty good, then that's great, but if not, then probably that is a signal that a little more reflection is needed. Could anything be done about the hours? Will the course get more interesting as it goes along? Are the drawbacks things you can live with and make work, or is there some action you need to take if you are not to let frustrations build up?

Sadly, in some ways, another time for reflection is when things have gone wrong, for example when there is a break up (was it my fault?) or if you don't get a job you wanted (what was wrong with my CV, or was it my interview technique?) It's equivalent to the 'post-mortem' of a match when a team doesn't win. At that time, we reflect because we need answers to the question, why weren't we successful? We do it to make sure we can make progress by identifying what caused the 'failure' and doing something about it.

"We do not learn from experience. We learn from reflecting on experience."
John Dewey

If you have been engaging with the activities in this book so far, you will have identified your dreams, goals and intentions, and started to make changes towards realising your dreams. As you progress, reflection is going to be a vital part of the journey. You need to check progress and see how far you've come. This serves several useful functions:

1. It gives you the chance to see that you have made progress (or not and we'll come to that in a moment). This can be very motivating and inspiring. Maybe you have learned new skills or made some important decisions.

2. It allows you to evaluate parts of that progress. Were some things easy and others much more difficult? Would you do the same thing as you did if you were faced with that same situation in the future?

3. If you haven't made the progress you wanted, then it gives you a chance to consider why. Were there specific obstacles or has time simply drifted by without action? How you respond will depend on what you consider in your reflection.

4. It gives you the chance to reaffirm that what you are moving towards IS what you want.

5. It builds in a process of accountability. If you set a goal that you aimed to achieve in a month – did you? Or have you done nothing whatsoever about it? If that is the case, that's

okay but it will be worth reflecting on the reason why and whether it is something you want to do? It is easy to say that time or busyness prevented it, but we usually make time for things we value and think are important. Remember, if you can easily forget your dream, then you need to ask yourself whether it is worthwhile.

Reflection is something that can be built into everyday life, and many people who do that say they live happier and more fulfilled lives as they make a point of taking stock and evaluating where they are – that means taking an active part in life not just being passive and letting it go by.

"Without reflection, we go blindly on our way, creating more unintended consequences, and failing to achieve anything useful."
Margaret L. Wheatley

How to be more reflective

As with so many things in life, learning to use reflection effectively takes time. But it is time well spent. People do this in all sorts of ways. Some will have a period each day when they can be alone with their thoughts and use mindfulness or meditation to free themselves of some of the mental busyness and clutter that can so easily prevent any reflection. Others will build in a weekly slot or even take themselves off for a day on a monthly or periodic basis specifically for reflection. Essentially, all you need is yourself and some peace and quiet. That's not to say you can't be reflective on a rush-hour train, but to begin with peace and quiet will make the process a little easier, and perhaps paper and pen or tablet will be helpful to make notes.

Think back to the example of the mirror. Sometimes you will look in it and think to yourself that you got it right – you look just how you wanted to look and no further action is needed, except perhaps to make a note to wear that outfit again! But at other times reflection will mean that changes are indeed necessary. Of course, this applies beyond the mirror example. Maybe your hope that the relationship you are worried about would improve isn't being realised. Maybe the promotion you were promised really doesn't look like it's ever going to happen. In those cases, some changes may be needed and allowing time for the process of reflection will help you to decide on what course of action you need to take to ensure your own happiness and fulfilment.

"Learning without reflection is a waste. Reflection without learning is dangerous."
Confucius

Activity 12

- Decide on a quiet place and allow yourself a bit of time to complete this activity.

- Look back at the dreams, intentions and goals you wrote down earlier.

- Even if it is just a few days, set aside some time to reflect on these dreams, intentions and goals.

- Do they still feel 'right' or would you like to reword or redefine them?

- If the answer is yes, then go ahead.

- If not, were there any steps which you had decided or intended to take by now?

- If you have taken those steps, then reflect for a few moments on each of them. Did you learn anything? Ask of each one, did that 'step' open up another one?

- If you haven't taken them, ask yourself if there was a valid reason, or was it that you simply did not get around to it?

- Note down any learning points or even just things you notice, and make any changes to the dreams, intentions or goals that you feel you need to.

Progress and accountability

Whatever you are working towards in any area of your life it is important to assess progress. Failure to do so means we can lose sight of our destination, or only make progress at a very slow rate, which in turn can lead to us feeling demotivated. Building in time for regular reflection will mean we can check we are progressing and adjust our planned 'route' according to our progress and learning.

One of the things that can help hugely with progress is having accountability. This can happen in a whole variety of ways. Employing a coach is perhaps one of the best methods of ensuring you get the accountability you need, but that will, of course, cost money. Alternatively, a supportive friend or partner or a business colleague may be able to help.

I've put below a few reasons why working with a coach, someone who is experienced in the areas you are working on and developing in, can be a good plan and actually accelerate progress towards your dreams and goals.

Coaching comes with a cost, but an investment in a professional relationship with someone who can bring skills to the table you can't access otherwise may be money well spent; and if any of the following apply to you, then NOT hiring a coach will also have a cost in terms of not getting where you want to be either in your life or in your business. In short, coaches are usually effective, and at least part of that is the process that happens when a person decides to hire a coach. Hiring a coach is itself a sign that you are hungry for change, and if you are prepared to pay for the service, which may involve significant cost, then it is likely that you are prepared to invest the time and effort as well as the money to make the necessary changes.

Like any other decision people make, the reasons a person might hire a coach are many and various, but here are a few of the common reasons that people decide on coaching. Have a read and see if any resonate with you.

Feeling 'stuck'

One common reason people have for hiring a coach is the feeling that they can't move forward with some particular aspect of their lives, a particular relationship perhaps, or in their business or perhaps one part of it. Common business reasons might be that they need to increase confidence to speak to large groups of people, learn to delegate effectively or learn to 'own' their expertise and authority. In people's personal lives it is often to do with relationships or learning to be assertive, more confident or maybe better at decision making. Sometimes people can feel trapped not by the situation but by the particular way they see it. Coaches are skilled at helping people see old things in new ways.

Going through a transition

Life is not static; in many ways it is a series of changes. People around us change, situations change and we as individuals change. Some people love change, even feel excited by it, but others feel very afraid of the whole process. Often, they value having someone on the outside who can ask the right questions to help them get a new perspective on the transitions and to deal with the emotions they feel, while continuing to move forward.

"A coach is someone who tells you what you don't want to hear, and you see what you don't want to see, so you can be who you have always known you can be."
Tom Landry

Needing vision

Others hire a coach because they may have vague ideas about what they want to achieve in their business or life but lack a really clear vision, which is an essential ingredient for success. A coach can help someone gain real clarity of purpose. Usually through asking questions, they can help you pinpoint how you want things to be, clarify your vision, and then work with you to establish the steps you need to take. So, if you struggled in the beginning identifying dreams and goals BUT know you are not happy with where you currently find yourself, then a coach may help.

Needing to develop skills

Some coaches will work with clients to develop a particular skill, perhaps having 'sales' conversations or giving presentations, possibly even being confident enough to talk to people at network meetings. Part of the coaching process is to identify what the client needs and then work together to develop what is needed. This might involve some signposting to other agencies or people but that would depend on the particular skills that need to be developed.

"Coaching is all about having someone believe in you and encourage you, about getting valuable feedback, about seeing things from new perspectives and setting your sights on new horizons."
Ellen DeGeneres

To change ways of working

As humans we are quick to develop particular ways of doing things, and even when these cease to serve us well, we can find it hard to change the ways we do things. Coaches can not only help in identifying these habits or ways of working, and the often-negative impact they may have, but they also can help people develop more effective practices.

To bring about shifts in mindsets

This is often one of the most effective ways of bringing about positive change in either business or life. By identifying the mindsets that hold you back, as we did in the early chapters of the book, and ridding yourself of those great progress can be made. So, if you struggled with that, it might be that some coaching could help. The coach can help you see the impact these mindsets can have on your life or business and, importantly, help you to replace these mindsets with alternative ones that will lead to greater success.

"Coaching is unlocking a person's potential to maximise their own performance. It is helping them to learn rather than teaching them."
Timothy Gallwey

A huge number of coaches exist, from general life, business or development coaches through to specialist relationship or mindset coaches. Coaching can take place individually or in groups and even by Skype or telephone. The specific qualification route of each coach may vary and so may their methods and ethos, but perhaps the most important thing if you decide to choose a coach is to make sure it is right for you.

To do that it is worth doing a bit of research about the programmes they offer, the delivery method and the cost. Coaching is not cheap and clearly you need to know what you are committing to and make sure that you can afford it before you sign up for it. The commitment is not just financial; it's also an investment of your time and effort, and unless you can commit to change, then it may not represent a good return on your investment.

Looking at testimonials or getting some personal recommendations may help, but perhaps the most important step is having some contact with the coach before you sign up for anything. Most coaches offer a free telephone or Skype introductory call, or even a free short exploratory session. It is important for the coach to get results, so many won't want to take you on as a client unless they feel they can help. I understand that coaching needs commitment, but if a coach wants you to sign away a lot of money before you have had some contact, I'd be wary. Perhaps it's a good time to listen to your intuition when it comes to deciding if a coach seems right for you.

In the next part of the book we are going to focus on how to make things happen, what you need to do and the habits you need to develop to lead a happier, more successful and fulfilled life.

PART 3
Making it happen

CHAPTER 9
Habits for magnificence

"We are what we repeatedly do. Excellence therefore is not an act but a habit."
Aristotle

Hopefully, we all know by now that developing the right mindset is crucial to success, happiness and fulfilment. But we can also work on certain habits that will help us on that journey, and even if they are things that don't come naturally at first, putting some effort into developing these will aid you on your journey towards fulfilling your goals and dreams. A habit is something we do regularly, so these will only be effective if they become part of a daily or weekly routine. If we just do them once then forget about them, they are unlikely to have much of an impact.

Here in this chapter are seven habits for magnificence you need to develop.

Seize each day

When you read biographies about people whose lives have been successful you find many of them will be 'early risers' who have very set routines to begin the day. There is nothing magical about working in the morning as opposed to at other times, BUT I know for myself the way in which I start the day has a bearing on the rest of the day and how it goes.

If you are going to do something that you love and are excited about, then it is natural to have more of a spring in your step; so I suppose if we take that one step further, if you start living a life you love, the chances are you will be excited by each new day. Think about that for a moment. Would life feel different if you achieved your dream and were working doing something you love, or feeling fulfilled in relationships? The way we approach each day says something about how we feel about our life in general.

Not only are we positive about getting up if we have exciting things to do but we prepare for them – we'll pack if we are going on holiday, we'll prepare if we are taking on a challenge. If you were to be running a marathon or beginning a challenge of some sort, you would probably start your day in a slightly different way than you would if you were just getting up to do a job you didn't like much anyway. If you are preparing for a marathon, there will be lots of days when getting up to train may be hard, I acknowledge that, but for now just think about the feeling you'd have when you are going to do something exciting or something you have spent some time preparing for. Harness that feeling for the moment.

"When you arise in the morning think of what a precious privilege it is to be alive – to breathe, to think, to love."
Marcus Aurelius

Part of seizing each day is making sure that YOU make decisions about how the day goes. Clearly, some things might happen that are beyond your control, but you can start by making a conscious decision about how you decide to start each day.

Start it right

Do you have an optimum time or way to wake up? Some people like to bounce out of bed as soon as their alarm goes off, others will like to snooze, and others might not even need an alarm. It doesn't really matter at all – go with what feels best, but generally we function better with a routine and no one can really get the day off to a great start if they feel rushed and hassled. Owning the day means beginning it on your terms. While there is no 'right' routine, it is important to make time for breakfast and ensure it is one which will benefit you – that is all part of looking after yourself, which is something we will come to in more detail later in Chapter 12. Some people like to fit in exercise in the morning, and others will enjoy spending time meditating and maybe setting specific intentions for the day. I find for myself that it is important to plan in some time in my morning routine to be present in the moment, to be mindful for a short time – that seems to have a big impact on how I go through the day.

The specific ingredients of a morning routine or ritual are probably less important than the routine itself, so work out what elements are important to you and then devise a start to your day that works for you and means that you appreciate each new day for the opportunities it brings and allows you to use it well.

Be the master of your time

I can't count how many times I have heard others (or myself!) grumble that there just isn't enough time. But let's be honest, we all get the same amount, though we may have differing demands on what we need to do in or with that time. What we can't change is the number of hours, minutes or seconds in a day. What we can change is our attitude to those and how we use them.

Often the problem is that we don't see time as the asset it is. The first step to using time more wisely is seeing how important it really is and then treating it like a precious commodity. There are some things we have little choice about in the short term. If you are in paid work, then you will simply have to be there for a certain number of hours each day. Even if you run your own business, there will always be certain things that must be done. But even accepting that, there are still a lot of hours and even more minutes that we choose to spend in particular ways.

Never forget about minutes. Have you ever NOT started something because you think you only have five minutes, but it turns out to be 20 minutes and you could have got the job done? When you start valuing your time you will find that you use even the five minutes while waiting for someone because even five minutes are valuable.

It is helpful to acknowledge the fact that YOU choose how you spend large amounts of your time each day. Even if you work nine hours a day (and there will often be breaks within that) that still leaves 15 hours where you decide what you do. Of course, a significant part of that will be devoted to sleep and you will need to eat, but you are in control of when and how you do those things as well as what you do with the remaining hours. Think about the last few days and how you have spent your time. Did you choose to spend an hour flicking through social media or did it 'just happen'? Did you choose to watch a film on television for two hours or did it just happen? There is nothing wrong with either of those things, but if there are things that you say are important that you aren't fitting in, then it is time to think about your priorities.

"The key is not to prioritize what is on your schedule but schedule your priorities."
Stephen Covey

Be clear about your priorities

Often, we will say what our priorities are yet end up doing completely different things. Is your health important to you? If yes, then it surely follows that fitting in time to exercise or eat well must be a priority. Are your personal relationships important? Well, quality time with the people you love and value must be a priority.

It is often helpful at the beginning of a week to plan in the big stuff, work, time with family, and make sure when you do that you also plan in some time to take care of yourself. Think about your specific goals for the week and plan time to do those. Also allow time for some reflection and for your own learning or inspiration to make sure you stay inspired or motivated.

When you have identified priorities then it is easier to make sure you fit them in, even if that means NOT doing other things. If your goal was to research something, then it may be the TV has to be turned off or an invitation turned down in order to get it done. If it is a priority, then that shouldn't be a problem.

"Action expresses priorities."
Mahatma Gandhi

Beware of multi-tasking. I think this is rapidly becoming a modern-day curse. Sometimes ten minutes of focused attention can be more fruitful than an hour of diluted, distracted 'work'. Not just work either; if you are spending time with a partner or friend, then spend time with them, put the phone away. I know we lead busy lives, but often we create the busyness by not simply attending to one thing at a time and finishing it, or by being distracted, so we may 'do' lots of things but not really be 'present' and attending fully to any moments through the whole day.

Remember to be realistic; you are human. When I have worked coaching people and they show me what they want to achieve, sometimes I am left wondering whether it is a mere mortal I am dealing with or a time-bending superhero! It is important to aim high and be aspirational, but there must be a degree of realism as well. The way you handle that will vary for everyone. Sometimes tasks need to be delegated or combined. Sometimes identifying one overarching priority helps, but the important thing to realise is that if you give yourself something that is unachievable, it will simply lead to dissatisfaction and probably you being very self-critical. This in turn usually leads to a lot of time-wasting as we can all enjoy a bit of a wallow in those situations.

Be proactive

When you grab hold of the day rather than letting it 'run' you then it is much easier to be proactive rather than reactive. Let's just take the example of emails. It may be that answering emails was not your priority for the day, but if you end up scrolling through them, then the chances are you will spend a considerable amount of time answering them rather than getting going on your priority tasks for the day. If it is a priority, then it deserves your best attentions. Now, every situation is different and sometimes answering emails IS the priority. The important point here is that you decide on your priorities then tackle them rather than allow yourself to be in the position of responding to other people's priorities.

"I believe that everyone chooses how to approach life. If you are proactive, you focus on preparing. If you are reactive, you focus on repairing."
John C. Maxwell

Stay motivated

We all have a reason why we do what we do – that is 'motivation'. We might exercise to get fit, work so that we get paid, work longer hours to get a bonus or overtime, or learn to gain a qualification. We always have a reason for what we do, whether conscious or unconscious. Many people feel very motivated when they start out on a plan but find their motivation wanes after a while. To maintain your motivation, it is helpful to build in the following:

- Remind yourself of your goals and your 'why'. Visual reminders are great – post-it notes, vision boards, a photo of where you want to go – it doesn't matter how you do it but keeping your goals in mind will help with motivation

- Take breaks away from the tasks. This is true for short term tasks and longer projects. All work and no play can decrease motivation. Allowing time for rest and to take care of yourself is vital, and often when we step away from something we get a clearer view and renewed motivation.

- Be inspired. Seek out people who inspire you, maybe people with similar goals or a coach or mentor. It can also be helpful to read stories that inspire you or nonfiction, podcasts or books, that can be an inspiration. Nature, art and creativity can be inspiring too, so work out what inspires you and take time to fit those things in on a regular basis.

Give yourself permission to say 'no'

This is an important habit to develop and one which can literally change your life. Some people, because they have mindsets that aren't helpful, find it tough to say no to anything or anybody. This might stem from a desire to keep everyone happy or feeling that others need looking after, or even a fear of criticism or rejection. But being able to say no is an important skill to develop.

"It's only by saying 'no' that you can concentrate on the things that are really important."
Steve Jobs

But saying no is not always easy. We can feel very guilty about it and sometimes others can make us feel guilty, possibly as a way of manipulating us. But saying no can be a powerful force for good. So, when you feel you want to say no just give yourself a minute to weigh the decision, thinking about the outcomes, immediate and longer term, that saying no would bring. Ensure you think about the realistic outcomes, not the worry of being judged in some way, and then don't ever be afraid to firmly and kindly say no. Imagine you are asked to stay late to work on a project at short notice. There will be times when you may decide it's the best thing to do – to help colleagues etc. – but there will be other times when you have other priorities. That is why being clear about priorities can make all sorts of other decisions easier.

As an individual, your needs are always a priority, not to the exclusion of others but not the reverse either. It is beneficial for all of us to live in a supportive, cooperative environment, but that doesn't mean that your own needs are unimportant.

Activity 13

For this activity I want you to think about the seven habits we've talked about in this chapter and which I've listed below. Consider each one in turn and assess the extent to which you already follow these habits, if you do, and the extent to which you need to develop them.

- Seize each day

- Start it right

- Master your time

- Be clear about your priorities

- Be proactive

- Stay motivated

- Give yourself permission to say 'no'

In the next chapter we are going to consider gratitude, kindness and positivity, which are further habits that will help you on the road to a fulfilling life.

CHAPTER 10
The power of gratitude

"Learn to be thankful for what you already have while you pursue all that you want."
Jim Rohn

In this chapter we are going to consider gratitude, kindness and positivity; but we can think of gratitude as being the foundation for the other two, and certainly the best way to start our discussion is by addressing gratitude itself. It has an amazing power to shift focus and literally make you see things very differently.

Quite simply, being grateful is great for us. Many of us may have grown up hearing things like 'count your blessings' or 'there's always a silver lining' or other exhortations to look on the bright side and focus on the good things, but when we actually do that it helps us in all sorts of ways.

In order to be grateful, we really must get in touch with where we are right now. So much of our lives can be lived looking to the future, or to the past, rather than actually being in the present. When that is the case, we rob ourselves of the pleasure of appreciating what we have. Take a moment wherever you are right now to just stop. Take a few deep breaths and connect with the present. Attend to the sensations you feel in your body. Are you warm or cold? Is the chair comfortable? Are you hungry or full? Often just taking a few moments to do that can help us focus on what we have. Hopefully, you'll have clothes that are comfortable, you may have had food or might be looking forward to a meal later, you might be sitting in a comfortable chair, and you might be glad to be indoors if it is raining outside. There may be a hundred other things we could be grateful for, but unless we give ourselves a moment, we can take them for granted. How brilliant it is to feel well! For anyone who has experienced significant illness, that is something that won't often be taken for granted again. Being healthy and pain-free is not something to be taken for granted.

That is one reason why building some time for stillness, meditation or mindfulness into every day can be very helpful. When we appreciate what we have then it can change our thoughts and feelings, and while we may still be pursuing other dreams, if we do so from a perspective of thankfulness, that 'energy' (think back to the law of attraction) will help us to attract more good things into our lives.

"Be thankful for what you have; you'll end up having more. If you concentrate on what you don't have, you will never, ever have enough."
Oprah Winfrey

By being grateful and appreciating what we have, we are more likely to be 'present' and that will in turn lead us to be more grateful by appreciating moments and what is around us rather than rushing headlong through every day. It begins to set up a healthy and helpful cycle of being ever more thankful. And ever more 'present'.

There is also evidence that being grateful helps us physically as well. Research undertaken by Dr Robert Emmons has shown how people who practise gratitude by keeping a gratitude journal exercised more and reported fewer physical symptoms. It is even thought to boost the immune system and lower blood pressure. Even those with neuromuscular disease experienced more high energy positive moods. But gratitude also seemed to help people attain more of their goals and be more positive. (You can find a summary of Emmons' work on gratitude and wellbeing here: https://emmons.faculty.ucdavis.edu/gratitude-and-well-being/)

"The real gift of gratitude is that the more grateful you are the more present you become."
Robert Holden

Not surprisingly, it can help us build and maintain positive relationships. At a simple level, it is usually easier to be around grateful people rather than those who constantly grumble; people want to spend time with positive happy people. That doesn't mean that it is never okay to talk about things that might have upset or disappointed you; what it does mean is that you make a choice whether to focus on the good, on the things you can be grateful for. When we are grateful we are also more likely to thank people for their contributions and that helps the wheels of friendship move more smoothly.

There may be some elements of personality involved, but we can all change, so even if it doesn't come naturally you can learn to be more grateful, and it will do you good.

Positivity

As shown in Emmons' work, people who were grateful were much more positive about their lives, in essence, happier. This shouldn't really be surprising. When you start focusing on the good things you will think differently and feel differently. Your outlook on the future will also change as you focus on the good possible outcomes not just the negative ones. Whatever genetics you were born with and whatever we have learned growing up or even in adult life, our brains retain some plasticity which means to a degree we can reprogram them; we can learn new ways of thinking.

If being positive has not come naturally to you in the past, it doesn't mean you can't decide to change and learn now how to be more positive. As with so many other aspects of our lives, we have a choice. We can choose to be positive and a good way to begin is by being grateful. Have you ever come across positive people and thought how their lives just seem easier? They seem to glide through life, and even when setbacks or challenges occur, they don't get derailed; they'll somehow manage to look on the bright side. Well, we can all be those people if we decide we want to be and take a few steps to manage our thinking. That's something we'll come back to in a later chapter too, but for now let's look at the link between gratitude and kindness.

Kindness

Robert Emmons' research has also shown that people who are grateful are also more likely to forgive others and be more helpful, generous and compassionate (https://greatergood. berkeley.edu/article/item/why _gratitude_is_good).

Most of us would probably not hesitate in agreeing that kindness is good. We probably all think we'd like to live in a kinder world and would want children to learn kindness. But just like gratitude, and quite apart from kindness benefiting the recipient, it is good for us too.

"You will never have a completely bad day if you show kindness at least once."
Greg Henry Quinn

In some ways, our level of happiness is determined by what we might call happy hormones, and obviously what happens to us, and how we respond and think about what happens to us, will have an impact on the levels of those hormones.

Strictly speaking, 'happy hormones' aren't all hormones. One of the chemicals you will have probably heard of as being responsible for happiness is serotonin, which is a mood-boosting neurotransmitter. Another is dopamine, another neurotransmitter, which drives our brains' rewards system.

Then there is oestrogen and progesterone. You'll all have heard of those hormones and know that an imbalance of these can cause irritability. Specifically, oestrogen is responsible in part for the formation of serotonin and it helps to keep our mood steady. Good levels of oestrogen protect us from irritability and anxiety. Progesterone too protects us from irritability and is also thought to have a role in helping us sleep well. Then there is something called oxytocin, which is both a hormone and a neurotransmitter and seems to have an impact on our levels of satisfaction. This particular one seems to have more of an impact on women than men. In addition, there are endorphins which can dull pain and increase our feelings of pleasure.

But it is also worth knowing about cortisol – often called the stress hormone. Cortisol is released in response to fear and stress, and prolonged high levels of it can have numerous negative effects on the body, such as lowering the immune system, increasing weight gain, interfering with learning and memory, and increasing the risk of depression and mental health problems.

Being kind releases serotonin, being empathic releases oxytocin, and the research of Dr Sonja Lyubomirsky found that people reported greater happiness when they are doing acts of kindness. In schools when 9-11 year olds were asked to do acts of kindness over a period of time, they became happier and also more popular (https://journals.plos. org/ plosone/ article?id = 10.1371/journal.pone.0051380).

Being grateful

I'm hoping we are now at the point where we can agree that being grateful is a good thing that will help us to be both more positive and kinder and that all of these will improve our level of happiness. So, how do we go about being grateful? Here's a few pointers:

- Regularly give yourself time to be still and focus on the present.

- Don't take anything for granted. If you had a good night's sleep in a comfortable bed that was warm and dry, there are several things to be grateful for – many homeless people would be so grateful for just that. If your basic needs for food, shelter and safety are met, then you have good reason to be grateful.

- Appreciate other people. If you have friends, family, colleagues or acquaintances, then be grateful. Loneliness is a growing problem in the UK, so if you have people around you that too is something to be very grateful for.

- Get out into nature. The world is a magnificent place and so often we don't appreciate it. Find ways to get out into nature or notice the nature around you; it's a great way of stimulating gratitude.

- Enjoy little things and appreciate them, whether that's a cup of coffee, a chat with a friend or time to relax and be with people you love.

Being grateful is a choice you can make, and if it is something that doesn't come very easily to you, then a good way to start is with a gratitude journal. That simply means deciding that each day you will find three things (or five or ten) to be grateful for and note them down. Doing this for just one week will make a difference. Instead of a journal it could be on a board or even collect notes in a jar or box – whatever works for you. One of the other great things about noting down what you are grateful for is that if you do have a day when your mood is low you can have a look at the things you have been grateful for and that will usually help raise your mood.

Being positive

"Being positive won't guarantee you'll succeed. But being negative will guarantee you won't."
Jon Gordon

Just like we can decide to be grateful, we can decide to be positive; it is something we can choose. Being grateful will help with this, so too will:

- **Spending time with positive people.** If you surround yourself with people who are negative, it will have an impact on your own mood. Some people we may have to spend time with, but if it isn't necessary then maybe spend less time with them.

- **Doing things you enjoy.** It doesn't have to be big things. Going for a walk, meeting a friend or reading a book can all help us feel more positive if they are things we enjoy.

- **Taking action so you feel you are moving forward with your goals.** As humans, we feel more positive when we see progress, and the feeling of getting stuff done is one we all usually enjoy.

- **Making sure you get the basics right.** I'll talk more about your self-care in Chapter 12.

- **Smile** – because apparently smiling can lower our blood pressure, even when the smile is a fake one! (http://www.cbsnews.com/news/even-a-fake-grin-may-help -lower-heart-rate-in-stressful-situations/) It can also boost the immune system (http://www.helpguide.org/articles/ emotional-health/laughter-is-the-best-medicine.htm).

- **Laugh.** It's not surprising that if smiling helps us emotionally and physically, then laughing will too. I must confess that in my opinion one of the best sounds on earth is that of children laughing. It is infectious and raises my spirits every time I hear it. It is hard to hear a person laughing without somehow ending up laughing yourself. Apparently, there are 15 muscles in the face alone that contract when we laugh, and as it spreads through the body many other muscles contract but then relax – some may become uncoordinated, so a really good giggle can make you unable to walk straight, for example. Our eyes water and in some ways our body becomes a bit out of control and, of course, we have all had the experience of irresistible giggles, especially in situations where we feel we shouldn't be laughing. It also influences our respiratory system and breathing becomes irregular but overall our oxygen intake increases. In many ways it is like a workout.

More about the power of laughter

"Laughing is and always will be the best form of therapy."
Dau Voire

Laughter can improve our mood and that can help if we feel anxious. I remember working in an Intensive Care Unit where there were times of massive tension and distress, and yet it was probably one of the jobs in which I laughed the most. This wasn't because we minimised the distress of our patients and family – quite the opposite; laughter was a release of the tension and anxiety that, as staff, we felt because it was a high-pressure setting. Over time laughter can help us all to become more resilient. The impact of laughter doesn't stop when we stop laughing; the positive effect on our mood can last for many hours. Laughing releases tension; in fact, when we are laughing muscles relax and stay relaxed for some time afterwards. But there is also evidence to suggest that laughter boosts our immune system and can even help improve heart health (the heart is after all a muscle) as it can increase blood flow. When we laugh we release endorphins – back to those happy hormones!

Laughter is contagious and it is fun. You may have seen a very popular video on social media recently which starts simply with one man on a train laughing and ends with everyone on the train laughing. People who laugh together are likely to work well as a team – somehow laughter creates a bond. If you walk into a party, or even a new office, you are likely to be drawn to people who laugh or smile rather than the ones who look depressed or down. Many of us will have had times when things may have looked bleak and the response would be either to cry or conversely to laugh. Amazingly, if we are able to choose the latter, often things start to look a little better straightaway because we start to feel more positive.

"There is nothing in the world so irresistibly contagious as laughter and good humour."
Charles Dickens

A good laugh helps reduce our levels of stress and, in fact, there is a new branch of therapy called 'laughter therapy'. Its aim is simple – to get you to laugh. Now, cynics reading this will probably be thinking that it can't be good for us if it is not genuine, but apparently the brain finds it tricky to distinguish between real and 'fake' laughter, so all the beneficial elements are there. And if we start out laughing in a slightly forced way, in fact, it quickly becomes real. A good burst of laughter will leave us feeling relaxed, buoyant and possibly exhausted – in effect it really is like a good workout.

Being kind

There are so many ways of being kind that it would be impossible to list them. The important thing is that we don't need to wait for opportunities to be kind. We can decide to be kind. We know it will have a positive impact on us, so why wait? – let's seek out ways to do it. As with other areas of life, when we make a decision or set an intention to do something opportunities will arise. Kindness gives us the power to change someone's day, and not only by doing big stuff; a smile or a kind word can help hugely. The actions are important, but adopting the right attitude means that you are more likely to spot moments and situations when you can demonstrate kindness.

I'd like to end this chapter with a quote from Helen Keller on gratitude. Helen Keller was born deaf-blind and was the first deaf-blind person to earn a Bachelor of Arts degree. This is one of her quotes on gratitude.

"So much has been given to me I have no time to ponder over what has been denied."
Helen Keller

CHAPTER 11
Making the right choices

"No matter what the situation, remind yourself 'I have a choice.'"
Deepak Chopra

"I am who I am today because of the choices I made yesterday."
Eleanor Roosevelt

I've heard a few times recently people saying things like, "I couldn't help it," "They made me do it," or "Well, it wasn't my fault; it was because…" Well, let's just set one thing straight. Unless someone literally has a gun to your head or is putting you under threat – you have a choice.

But I also understand that it doesn't always **feel** like we have much of a choice. So, let's look at some strategies we can use to ensure that we are always aware that we are in control of our own actions and so can always exercise a choice about those, even if we can't choose some of the things that are happening to us or around us. In fact, lots of things can happen that we have no control or choice over, but even then we can exercise control of our response – we can make a choice.

The steps below will help everyone be able to be more aware that we can always make a choice and that actually those choices will have an impact on our future.

Take time to react

It happens to all of us; people upset or hurt us, stuff happens that makes us angry or unhappy, and of course it is a very human response to react. However, when we have lots of emotions our reaction may not be measured and sometimes we might make a situation worse by reacting when we are 'emotional'. It might not be easy, but just giving yourself a moment, even just a few seconds, can mean that we are better able to choose to react in a different way. Yes, it might make us feel instantly better in the short term to throw something, or yell at someone, or make a rude gesture when driving, but usually it doesn't really help the situation. In fact, sometimes it can make it a whole lot worse. So, give yourself a minute, take a deep breath and then choose how you will react.

Don't be influenced by others

I was talking with someone recently who was embroiled in a long and difficult legal battle. During the conversation, I asked why she had initially decided to take this route when it seemed to be there would have been other options. She suggested that a couple of friends had persuaded her as it wasn't right to let her adversary 'get away with it'. I don't think her friends meant to be unhelpful or give bad advice, but of course they weren't having to live through the consequences of the action. So, be cautious about accepting advice from people who won't have to accept the consequences of YOUR action. This is one of the occasions where learning to listen to your intuition might be really helpful. I expect she was, at the time, unsure about following their advice. Even if you ask for advice from others, it is always up to you whether you decide to act upon it – or not.

Think about the consequences

The advantage of taking even just a minute before you react is that it means you can consider the consequences of what you feel like doing, and sometimes that will be enough to help you to make a different choice. I'm confident that there won't be anyone reading this who doesn't regret some consequence of a choice they made or an action they once took. Of course, some consequences may be unforeseen, BUT if we stop for a moment, many could be anticipated and often a different reaction can avoid some unfortunate consequences.

"I believe that we are solely responsible for our choices, and we have to accept the consequences of every deed, word, and thought throughout our lifetime."
Elisabeth Kubler-Ross

Choices are cumulative

Sometimes the impact of choices won't be seen immediately, but over time they can have a big impact. Think about a person who makes a choice to overeat. We've all done it and the consequences if it is an occasional choice may not be great, but if this is a repeated choice then this will impact on your weight and probably your health. Similarly, if we always make the 'safe' choice and refuse to take a risk, never straying out of our comfort zones, the long-term impact may be that we significantly restrict our personal growth.

"It's our choices that show who we truly are, far more than our abilities."
J. K. Rowling

Feelings are NOT choices

People, if I ask them about a choice they have made, will often refer to feelings. But feelings, while they are real and can have a great influence upon us, are not choices or actions. We have feelings, but we can still choose how we act or react. Imagine someone who is feeling very sad, maybe they have suffered a disappointment or loss. The feelings might be awful, but the feelings don't make you stay in bed all day or snap at everyone – they are choices we make. Maybe they're not always conscious choices; sometimes our level of emotion means we react in certain ways, but usually we are aware of our emotional temperature, unless we have a problem with emotional regulation. If so, with insight into our own reaction we can learn to manage times when emotions may be intense. Managing emotions like stress and worry are an important part of taking care of ourselves and we'll look more at that in the next chapter.

Our choices will be influenced by our emotions but only to the extent we allow that, unless the emotion is very intense. So, if you are particularly afraid of something you may 'panic' in certain situations and therefore behave in out-of-character ways, but only if the fear is extreme. Feelings never 'make' us do things. We can still choose how we act even when we are experiencing extreme emotions.

The good news is that whatever life is throwing at us, and at times it might be pretty grim and we might feel battered by what is happening, we always have a choice, which means that we are not victims. Understanding that we can exercise choice empowers us to choose the life we want in all sorts of ways.

Putting our choices into action

Knowing something is a choice and even knowing which choice we want to make, doesn't mean that it is always easy to implement. Think about deciding to go to the gym first thing in the morning. You probably have a clear reason why you are planning to go, you may have packed your kit the night before and set your alarm for the right time, but then when it goes off you have to almost revisit that choice by getting out of bed, and it is at that point other factors and our feelings about those influence us. For example, if it's raining or if we feel especially tired, we may feel less keen; if we've had a text which means we may need to get a job done particularly early, then we may choose not to go.

The same is true with our thoughts, words and other aspects of behaviour, and we explored this in Chapter 3. Remember many of our negative thoughts will stem from our belief system and mindset. Doing some work on those may make it much easier to make the right choices, and that's something you may need to do on a repeated basis if negative or unhelpful thoughts keep invading your mind.

One of the things that can help us when it comes to choosing our thoughts and actions is making sure that we limit the negativity that can creep into our lives from a whole variety of sources. So, it is wise to run a bit of a check on what we put into our minds in terms of what we read, watch or listen to. But often negativity can come from people and this can cause the greatest conflict when it comes to people we care about, the very people we hoped would support us.

"Your mind will give back to you exactly what you put into it."
James Joyce

Choosing to limit negativity

If it is people we care about that are bringing negativity into our lives, then in most cases we need to learn how to enjoy our relationships without letting their negativity diminish us. There may be a whole host of reasons why those that you are close to can't seem to get behind your plans or dreams. Maybe they are jealous or resentful. Maybe they are simply worried because they don't want you to experience failure. But whatever their reasons, you have to accept that their comments stem from where and who they are. The important thing is to not let their negativity have an impact on your plans. That is not the same as having a reasoned discussion about pros and cons, where supportive friends may help you think about things from different perspectives, which can be helpful. This is about attitudes. Some people just seem to love to be negative.

Resist the urge to argue

Argument is not quite the same as a discussion, or even debate. An argument IS a discussion or debate, but the term implies a degree of conflict. Often it is easy to argue or debate issues we feel passionately about BUT which are a little distant from us. To argue about things we hold dear with people we hold dear will often cause considerable emotional upset. The fact is we are all unique individuals and therefore will see things differently. But arguing takes energy, and frankly you will rarely change opinions through argument, so accept that their stance is different from yours and do not waste energy trying to justify your opinions or decisions.

Put in some boundaries

The thing is, your dreams, wishes and plans need a bit of nurturing, and if you are forced into a situation where you end up having to defend or rationalise your dreams, then the time has come to limit how often you have to do that. I am not saying don't see the person, but if seeing them saps you of energy to pursue your dreams, then either see them less OR when you see them make sure that your plans are not up for discussion. There may be all sorts of reasons why they don't see things the same way that you do, and think that you shouldn't go travelling, expand your business, retrain, move house or whatever it is, but if that is what you want to do, then you need people around you who can be positive about your plans.

Cherish your dream

When faced with any kind of doubt it is easy to lose heart, so make sure you spend time cherishing your own dreams and plans, especially in the face of negativity from others. How do you do this? Start by reminding yourself why you have that dream in the first place, visualise what achieving it will mean for you, and keep on taking those steps you know you must in order to reach your goal. Also, take time to surround yourself with positive folk, people who are rooting for you to get where you want to go.

Above all, get busy

And the bottom line is this: the crucial part of achieving anything, pretty much, is actually doing something! Somehow activity sends a powerful message both to ourselves and others. It certainly is a good way to show the people who doubt you that you are serious. But it also has a really positive impact on our own subconscious. With action our dreams are not just vague thoughts, but something real. This creates a positive momentum. And it will make it easier to choose the positive thoughts over the negative ones.

"What you do speaks so loudly that I cannot hear what you say."
Ralph Waldo Emmerson

If necessary, 'fake it to feel it'

Having goals can help in taking action, but there will still be times when you don't feel like doing what you've decided to do or what at least part of you knows you should. Well, when that happens, which it almost certainly will, it might be the right time to simply fake it!

"Don't fake it till you make it, fake it till you become it."
Amy Cuddy

As humans, there are times when we have to do things or 'be' a certain way even when it is the last thing we feel like doing or the last way we want to be. In general terms authenticity is important in business, in relationships and in life, but there will always be times when we end up having to fake it in some respect. It is not necessarily a bad thing as by actually getting on and doing or even 'being' a particular way we can then muster up the particular feelings we need.

In more general terms, there is a scientific basis for the 'fake it to feel it' mentality. Research by Harvard Business School professor Amy Cuddy found that standing in a 'power pose' was likely to make you feel more confident. We would probably all be able to acknowledge that on those occasions when we really haven't felt like doing much at all that if we do muster the effort to slap on a smile and get through the day, by the end we are likely to feel better.

This is because the act of moving our muscles into a smile starts a feedback loop to the brain and then we start to feel better.

Of course, a lot of what we do starts with our thoughts, but while we all know we can control our thoughts – though it may be hard at times – we also know that if we can't, that doesn't mean we have to act the way our thoughts tell us. We can choose to override those thoughts. For example, we may feel angry if we have been upset by someone, but we may make a conscious choice not to act on those thoughts, if only because of the consequences. If you displayed an angry response every time someone irritated you, you'd probably be unlikely to keep a job for very long, for example. So, we know that we don't have to act the way we feel. As we said at the start of the chapter, we always have a choice.

"It is easier to act yourself into a new way of thinking than it is to think yourself into a new way of acting."
A. J. Jacobs

Every time we try something new, or perhaps work in a new role, there will be things we have to do or tasks we need to perform that we probably don't feel very confident about. But when we do them, usually more than once, we gradually become more confident in our abilities and see that we can quickly acquire new expertise. It is the act of doing that changes our feelings and therefore our thoughts; eventually we start to think more positively about those skills or situations.

What we can take from that is that doing is perhaps more powerful in changing our beliefs than thinking.

"You must be the person you have never had the courage to be. Gradually, you will discover that you are that person, but until you can see this clearly, you must pretend and invent."
Paulo Coelho

How to fake it till you feel it

Here's a few helpful tips for those occasions when you find you have to fake it, remembering that this should be just a step along the way; to be constantly faking it would mean that you would lose authenticity, and if there are underlying issues that are stopping you feel the way you want to, then it is best to think about how these can be sorted out.

1. **Remind yourself of your strengths.** As humans, we somehow find it very easy to focus on our weaknesses, on all the things we can't do, rather than what we can do or what we have achieved.

2. **Decide to be optimistic.** Nothing saps confidence as much as thinking about all the things that can go wrong rather than thinking about the good outcomes, the things that could go right. Decide to focus on those.

3. **Know your own body.** We project ourselves through our bodies, and if someone is nervous, they will hunch their shoulders or be tense. Put some effort into getting to know how you 'look' in different situations, then work at creating a

different image for those times when you need to, practise a powerful pose, and get used to standing tall even if you don't feel like it.

4. **Dress to impress … yourself**. Many of us would acknowledge that when we wear certain clothes we feel different. I know many homebased workers who tell me they work differently when they dress as if they were going out to work than they do when they dress in comfy stay-at-home clothes. This will not be the same for everyone, of course, so it is important to get to know yourself. In many ways, when we fake it we are convincing ourselves that we 'can' do whatever needs doing, so anything that helps with that process will be effective.

5. **Look outside yourself.** Having said that we need to understand ourselves, we also need NOT to become too self-obsessed. Concentrating on others can help us to get a better perspective. I remember once going for an interview and seeing a woman fall just as I approached the building. I spent several minutes helping her and, of course, my nerves vanished and I felt more confident.

In the next chapter we are going to focus specifically on how you can take care of yourself.

CHAPTER 12
Taking care of you

If you take one message from this book, let it be this:

You are of value and that means that taking care of you needs to be a priority. It is not indulgent; it is essential.

This applies to both your physical and mental wellbeing. The two are, of course, connected; looking after your physical wellbeing will help towards your mental wellbeing.

This term mental wellbeing describes our mental and emotional state – which of course might change from day to day, and even several times within the day.

Although we are all individuals with unique personalities, people with good mental wellbeing tend to feel confident and have a good level of self-esteem; they are usually able to express emotions appropriately, not in ways which may hurt or damage themselves or others, and are generally able to cope with the ups and downs of life and the stresses it can bring. They are also able to work and live productively and enjoy relationships with others.

I am concentrating here on maintaining wellbeing rather than addressing specific problems which may require professional help.

The format of the rest of this chapter is a little different from the others. It's a listing of ten things you can and should be doing to take care of yourself followed by an activity aimed at creating your own action points for bringing them into your life.

I've recorded a short video to accompany the list if you'd like to watch that too: https://youtu.be/9cTBBBU3g7A. (Please do subscribe to my YouTube channel too as I plan to add a lot more videos.)

1. Get the right fuel

Diet is important to wellbeing. Make sure you eat a balanced diet which is low in processed food and sugars. Make a determined effort to get your five (or even better seven) portions of fruit and veg each day and drink plenty of water. Be careful too that you don't use alcohol, drugs or nicotine to elevate your mood – it may help for a short time but will not be a lasting solution.

2. Exercise

When we exercise our bodies some 'feel good' hormones are released into our bloodstream, so actually our mood improves. It might be hard getting out of the door, but you nearly always feel better afterwards – though you may be exhausted! Almost any exercise will help, but obviously if you choose something you enjoy, that will be all the better. And make sure you take steps to look after your body, have the right equipment etc. and be aware of your safety.

3. Get enough sleep

We are probably all aware that when we are tired it can impact on our mood, so getting enough sleep generally (we can all survive a few days of being extra busy) will help us 'feel' better.

If we are exercising regularly, that will also help us with our sleep.

There are some useful tips on how to get a good night sleep here: https://hubpages.com/health/6-Easy-Steps-To-A-Good-Nights-Sleep

4. Have a routine

Some people feel that it is routine that can make them feel low and although we all benefit from a holiday or a change occasionally, there is a lot to be said for having a routine. It will often help to ensure we fit in the things we need to take care of ourselves.

5. Allow time for your relationships

Humans are social beings, and most people function best when they have good social contacts with others and feel they have people who they trust and who can support them. Some people function well with just a few good friends, whereas others may need more social contacts to feel at their best, but we all need some. Isolation and loneliness are linked to low mood, so make sure you build in opportunities to spend time with people – it's not a luxury; it is essential.

6. Embrace positivity

Developing a positive outlook can help maintain wellbeing. It seems to be something that some people find easier to do than others, but something everyone benefits from. Often it is a question of deciding to focus on the good, on the things that are going well, the things you can be grateful for. It might take a bit of effort at first, but it will pay dividends in the long run. You can follow me on Instagram for a regular dose of positivity: https://www.instagram.com/sheilamulvenney

7. Prioritise yourself (learn to say no)

It is important to take care of yourself; that means making time for things that are important to you, friends or hobbies, or time just to relax. Sometimes that means we have to say 'no' to other things, but even if you feel like you have a lot of conflicting responsibilities, it is still important to look after yourself, so you need to give yourself permission to put yourself first sometimes. You'll find some useful tips here:

https://successstory.com/inspiration/ways-to-take-care-of-yourself

8. Challenge yourself

Achieving something is good for all of us. The satisfaction that comes from learning something new or trying a new hobby is good for your mental wellbeing, as long as it doesn't stress you out too much!

It's also a good idea to make sure you always have some things to look forward to – not just big things like holidays but meetings with mates or trips to do things that you enjoy.

9. Learn to live in the moment

One of the things that can be very harmful to mental wellbeing is worry or anxiety. There may be loads of things at any one time we could worry about, but it rarely achieves anything positive. Developing strategies to manage anxiety will help. Perhaps try mindfulness. You can find a few useful starter exercises here: http://attunededucation.com/2017/03/14/4-mindful-exercises-to-try-today/

Meditation and yoga can also help, as can being in nature (a great stress reliever in itself). There are also a lot of 'apps' that can help you relax and slow your breathing and help focus on the here and now.

10. Develop personal resilience

Life will always present us with challenges, but if we can develop resilience, then when it does it is less likely to have a damaging impact on our mental wellbeing. So, get to know the things that stress you and what you can do to relieve that stress and make sure you 'practise'. Life's challenges are far less likely to cause damage when we have armed ourselves with strategies that we know will help us. You'll find some useful advice here too: https://hubpages.com/health/5-Easy-Ways-to-Become-Emotionally-Robust

Activity 14

So, now that you have read all these steps you can take to maintain your wellbeing, this activity is about applying them to your life. I'm sure you're already doing some, but here's where you can consider where you can make further improvements.

Write out a "Personal Wellbeing Plan" headed with your name and the date.

Under the heading "Strengths", from the ten areas identify the ones which you see as areas of strength, so if you exercise regularly, that is a strength.

Have a think about the areas where you would like to improve and, under the heading "Areas to work on", make a note of those areas.

Taking care of your own mental wellbeing is up to you. Under the heading "Action points", write out a statement about why you want to take care of yourself and a list of the steps you plan to take to see that you do.

PART 4
Coping with challenges

CHAPTER 13
Dealing with disappointment

"The size of your success is measured by the strength of your desire, the size of your dream, and how you handle disappointment along the way."
Robert Kiyosaki

Disappointment is something that will happen to almost everyone in life. But even when we've experienced it before, it is something we may find hard to handle the next time we have to face it. However, as humans we are resilient and although it may sometimes take us time to recover, we can all metaphorically pick ourselves up, dust ourselves down and carry on.

The size of the disappointment will have an impact on how we react, but most of it is down to how we frame it. Do we see it as a temporary setback or as something we will never recover from? Some people find amazing resilience and determination in coming back from disappointment and tragedy to continue pursuing their dream.

The tennis player Petra Kvitová had the fingers of her racquet hand slashed during an attack in her home yet competed once again in high-level tennis, even though many had doubted that would be possible – a testament to her courage and perseverance.

Using some of the strategies we have already discussed will help, reminding yourself of your dream and your 'why', being positive and checking in regularly with your thoughts.

One of the main problems that can arise when there is disappointment is it somehow touches our fear of failure. Failing doesn't feel nice, but it is bound to happen at some time. The important thing is to see it for what it is and not let it soak into our inner being. We need to make sure we check our mindset and do things that will help us stay positive and confident and not let us wallow. Part of that process is learning not to listen to that inner critic that we all have – so, let's look at some ways we can silence that critical voice.

Our inner critic can keep us safe by being a reality check. But like a lot of essentially helpful things, if it goes unchecked, it can cause damage, lowering our confidence and self-esteem, preventing us from doing new things or putting ourselves outside of our comfort zone, and in all sorts of ways making us feel less happy. Sometimes, especially after a disappointment, it can get us into a terrible downward spiral.

Listen

"Be aware of the negative self-talk and listen in with curiosity and compassion instead of guilt and shame."
Elise Museles

I know it sounds counterintuitive but to 'fight back' and silence that voice you first need to take notice of what it is saying. Often our response is to try and ignore it, but that can be incredibly hard to do as it keeps chattering on in the background. Take a moment to identify what it is actually saying and then you can launch your counter-arguments. Some people find it even helps to write some of the 'accusations' down and then deal with them.

State some truths

Clearly what you reply with will depend on what is being said. Back it up with universal truths, you are of value, people love you, what you think and feel matters, your opinion counts, and so on, the sort of truths we discussed in Chapter 4. After a disappointment, it will usually focus on the way you messed things up, and if you don't reject some of the criticism, you will find it can rob you of your confidence, so some timely reminders about all the other things that have happened which were down to you could help to silence it.

"If you gave your inner genius as much credence as your inner critic, you would be light years ahead of where you now stand."
Alan Cohen

Insist on kindness

What amazes me about our inner critic is that we allow a part of us to treat us and speak to us in a way we would never speak to others. If that voice is saying, "Wow, you made a right mess of that," imagine if you would say that to a friend in your situation. I'm sure you wouldn't. Nine times out of ten you would be kind even if critical. It seems we have a wealth of compassion when dealing with others but can be short of it when it's our own internal critic. So, be sure to treat yourselves the way you would treat others. When you ask yourself if you would say the sorts of things your inner critic is saying to you and the answer is 'no', then quite simply you need to stop listening.

"Your inner critic is getting in the way of all those great things, which you deserve and are meant to accomplish. Drown out that negative voice with a louder, more powerful voice. A voice that believes in you and defends you, encourages you and loves you."
Trina Hall

Get busy

The problem with our inner critic is that it can convince us NOT to do things and a sure-fire way to shut that voice up is to get on and do 'it' – whatever 'it' might be. In more general terms, getting busy, productive and creative will usually turn down the volume of that inner critic if not silencing it completely. When you do get busy it does need to be with something that will occupy your mind, so that in effect you squeeze out the voice, or something directly related to what it is saying. If it is saying you are hopeless with people, then go and meet up with some mates. If it is saying that you won't get a job you are going for, then throw yourself into some reading or research so that you are just too busy thinking about other things to give it any room at all.

One of the things that really gives traction to the inner critic is a fear of failure. It is entirely normal and like other fears can be dealt with.

"If you hear a voice within you saying 'you cannot paint,' then by all means paint and that voice will be silenced."
Vincent Van Gogh

Using and losing the fear of failure

Some people's lives have been strangled not by failure but by the FEAR of failure. A fear of failure will stop us stepping out of our comfort zone, trying new ventures – in case they don't work, embarking on a relationship – in case we get hurt, or applying for a new job – in case we don't get it. There isn't one area of life that is unaffected for a person who is afraid of failure. We don't go around saying that we aren't doing something because we are afraid of failing; we tell others, and sometimes ourselves that we don't really want whatever it is and that we are happy as we are, but even as the words come out of our mouth part of us knows that is simply not the case. While elements of this will be evident throughout our lives, if we have faced disappointment, it is likely to be a lot worse for a time. But forewarned is forearmed!

"Only those who dare to fail greatly can ever achieve greatly."
Robert F. Kennedy

Responding to failure

Sometimes failure is a message – but not always. Thinking back on some occasions I had an experience of failure, sometimes it made me rethink certain actions, behaviours or plans, but on other occasions the experience of failure made me more determined. When I failed my driving test, for example, I waited a while, had some more lessons and passed. Sometimes failure and disappointment are great teachers, if we are prepared to learn.

"I've not failed. I've just found 10,000 ways that won't work."
Thomas Edison

The important thing is not to see failure as central to yourself. Not passing an exam, not getting a job, the break-up of a relationship, these are all aspects of your life; they are not YOU. They may have an impact, sometimes profound, but they are not you. The experience of failure or disappointment can act as a springboard to success. What is important is how we 'frame' the disappointment or failure and what we do next.

"There's only one thing that makes a dream impossible to achieve: the fear of failure."
Paulo Coelho

Fear can be a useful emotion, but not if it stops you taking action, trying new things or taking a few risks.

Sometimes a fear of failure stems from a previous experience of failure – maybe you felt ashamed that you couldn't somehow come up to the mark or measure up in some way. But whose 'standard' were you trying to achieve and who exactly was measuring? Often if you look back, you may have failed because you were being pushed into a position that you didn't want anyway, trying to achieve something that you had not invested in yourself.

But if you delve below that, you usually find the bottom line in terms of the fear of failure is rooted in a concern about what others think. Obviously, we want the people we care about to care about us, but the likelihood is that whether we fail or succeed they will still care about us. As for the rest of the world, you need to ask yourself is their opinion really very important? Fear of failure is like any other fear generated by our subconscious minds and can be handled in a similar way.

Getting rid of the fear of failure

To get rid of the fear of failure you need to change your belief system and mindset about failure, increase your confidence and begin to take risks. Sometimes it is necessary to revisit instances of failure, reframe our memories and accept ourselves as we are.

If we can do this, then the opinion of others becomes far less important and we can be freed from the tyranny of worrying about what others think of us, which is so often at the root of a fear of failure.

"It's failure that gives you the proper perspective on success."
Ellen DeGeneres

Give yourself time

But sometimes following a disappointment we do need to give ourselves a bit of time to recover, not wallow but dust ourselves down before continuing our journey towards the life we want to live.

We live in a culture that places a high value on work, strength and courage. Characteristics like determination and the ability to keep going are highly regarded, which of course is good in many ways. The danger is that sometimes we are so determined to behave in the way we think our society tells us we should that we ignore some of the signals our own body or mind are sending to us.

Think about a small child falling over and hurting themselves. Obviously, what you want is for them to pick themselves up and dust themselves off and go back to what they were doing. BUT sometimes they need a few minutes before they can do that. So, they sit on a knee, they have a hug, or they may leave the 'crowd' for a moment and sit with a parent. They need to just take a little time before they are ready to get back into the game.

In general, though not always, for small children the 'catastrophe' is minor. They fall and get a shock, scrape a knee or bruise themselves. With adults often the 'fall' is much harder and more complex.

Adults (and, of course, sometimes children) cope with all sorts of disappointments and stress. We might have to handle difficult relationships, illness in our family or ourselves, problems with money, worries about redundancy, work difficulties including perhaps bullying or even discrimination at work, to mention just a few.

Sometimes the right response to a problem is to dust ourselves off and get back up again, but sometimes we need more than a minute if we are really to deal with issues in a way which doesn't store up problems for ourselves later.

Recently I overheard someone saying to their travelling companion that a mutual friend had been 'just marvellous'. Why? Because in the whole period of her sister's life-threatening illness she hadn't missed one day of work. Clearly it depends on severity, but keeping going when we are facing major difficulties, very stressful events, loss or other difficulties may well just mean we are storing problems up for the future.

Why do we feel like we must keep going even after a disappointment or failure? In short, it is what we have been told we must do. There are many messages we have all heard about being strong and carrying on. Just think about how many sayings we have that give that very message, 'keep a stiff upper lip', 'when the going gets tough, the tough get going' and 'the show must go on' to mention just a few.

We live in a society where to ask for help or to give a message that we need support can often be regarded as weakness, which couldn't really be further from the truth. Very often the people who appear strong may simply be pushing problems away or squashing them down rather than dealing with them.

"To share your weakness is to make yourself vulnerable; to make yourself vulnerable is to show your strength."
Criss Jami

What should we do?

The first step is to acknowledge that some things are difficult or stressful to deal with. It is our vulnerability that makes us human. Life for most people involves some stress, but most of us are resilient most of the time. We need to identify our support and when necessary ask for help – this isn't weakness.

If the situation is beginning to have a physical or mental impact upon you, then it may be that it is time to 'stay down' for just a short time to allow yourself a bit of recovery time.

We looked earlier at some of the often-repeated sayings we have and I'm sure we'll have all heard about the 'stitch in time'. By acknowledging that you have 'fallen over' or are at risk of having a fall, whatever the nature of that may be, then the sensible approach is to just give yourself a proverbial minute, because you are of value and because very often you will be supporting others.

People rest when they run a marathon and every fitness training programme requires periods of rest within it. It might be a holiday, a day to yourself or a few 'duvet' days, but whatever it is some time out to recover is essential. Allowing yourself time isn't wallowing; it is sometimes essential. Every disappointment is different and the impact will be different for every individual.

But even if we allow ourselves some recovery time, there will always come a time when we need to get back up and make sure that the disappointment or failure doesn't prevent us from moving forward with our dreams. Next time you face a disappointment or failure try these steps:

- Acknowledge what has happened and be honest about how that 'feels'.

- Often it can help to talk this through with someone – and maybe allow some recovery time.

- Express any emotion you need to.

- If self-critical thoughts appear in your mind, then reject them by stating things you know to be true.

- Reflect on the experience to see if there are things you can learn about yourself or your skills.

- Get busy doing what you need to do to fulfil your goals.

CHAPTER 14
Putting an end to procrastination

It's perhaps easy for us to know what we want to achieve, and breaking that down into manageable steps might also have been straightforward, but some people find there are some 'steps' that just don't seem to happen. Often this is referred to as procrastination: we know we should do something, part of us WANTS to do it, BUT there are a seemingly endless number of ways we can somehow not do it.

Whatever the task OR whatever the reason why we think we aren't doing it, there are usually just a handful of drivers or subconscious motivations that make us not do the things in question – and once you can put your finger on what those drivers are you can pretty much sort the problem out once and for all.

So, let's jump right in with some of the most common drivers for procrastination!

Fear of failure

"The greatest barrier to success is the fear of failure."
Sven Goran Eriksson

But we know how to deal with this, right?

The thing about action is that we sort of nail our colours to the mast. We make a statement somehow, whether it's choosing an image for our brand, writing a blog, talking to someone on the phone or designing a poster or lead page – as entrepreneurs we put ourselves out there. This is true in the personal areas of life too. Often the reason we procrastinate is because we are afraid of failure. Maybe we fear rejection; in not applying for a new job or training course maybe we are afraid we won't quite make the grade. Be aware that even when you feel that you have dealt with your fear of failure, it is likely to rear its head again when you make progress or have to step outside of your comfort zone in another way.

Fear of success

"Our deepest fear is not that we are inadequate. Our deepest fear is that we are powerful beyond measure. It is light not our darkness that frightens us. We ask ourselves who am I to be brilliant, gorgeous, talented, fabulous? Actually, who are we not to be."
Marianne Williamson

We have mentioned this before, and it is something ma
subconsciously afraid of. In our conscious mind we ma
to be successful, but in our subconscious we might b
that people may no longer like us, that we will be critic
we will somehow be a fraud or any one of a numbe
things. Others have a mindset that might say they wi
successful or that success doesn't happen for peopl
But like a fear of failure, this can be dealt with by

truth about you and affirming these truths rather than the unhelpful mindsets around success that you may have had. Once you start being honest with yourself about what your dreams are and working towards them it is not unusual to have a nagging doubt that success is something that is a bit frightening.

Lack of discipline

Others find that as soon as they have a list, or they set themselves a goal, they somehow can't get around to doing it. Or more commonly they do one thing then find they can't get around to the rest. It's almost an act of rebellion, against themselves. There may be elements of the above fears OR it maybe that there is an underlying mindset that somehow to conform to rules and lists and a specific programme is NOT a good thing. If you believe you are lazy and never finish ything, well it won't be surprising to find you are lazy and r finish anything. Hopefully, if you have worked through ook from the beginning, then you will have a good idea of ur unhelpful mindsets were and have got used to your thoughts so they don't derail you.

non either for people to be paralysed by a fear g thing. Often this subconscious motivation ion when they have made a decision that and has perhaps had some unwished-for effectively stop action in its tracks. And have made some decisions that with n't the best, because we are after all

ny are
y want
e afraid
sed, that
t of other
ll never be
e like them.
checking the

Desire for perfection

This might often be linked to a fear of regret BUT striving for perfection makes procrastination inevitable. Most things could be better; we could write a better blog, respond to a query more fully, write an email more carefully, prepare more fully for a phone call, or spend just a bit more time preparing a presentation – always that will be the case. But what successful people tend to do is DO! They take action, they do something; it might not be perfect, but the book that goes on being edited and is never published will simply never make it onto the bestseller list!

Understanding the reasons behind your procrastination means you are halfway to overcoming it. The next bit is easy – make an agreement with yourself to:

- **Remember your big picture**. What's your vision? Why do you want what it is you are striving for? This is a great motivator and a great antidote to procrastination.

- **Be honest with yourself.** If lists turn you off, then don't write a list. Find a different approach; even if it is just one thing you do each day, this will chip away at your predisposition to procrastinate (to find ways of not doing things).

- **Don't be hard on yourself**. In many ways it doesn't matter why we do what we do, but if it causes us a problem, then we need to sort it out. Fretting about it and giving ourselves a hard time about it will probably make it easier to procrastinate because we can use the time to beat ourselves up. **So just don't.**

- **Believe in yourself and your success**. The truth is that every one of us can change – it might not be easy, but we

159

can, and if you want to change this behaviour then you must first believe in the fact that you can.

DO IT ANYWAY

One of the other things that can prevent you getting on with it and doing it anyway is worry.

It is a natural emotion, one almost everyone will have experienced but one that many people find hard to deal with. We have probably all had nights when we have woken up with our minds full of worrying thoughts or been unable to prepare for an exam or event adequately because of worry. That is the irony of it: worrying can stop us getting done what we need to get done.

Also, we all know that worry doesn't usually help the situation, it will stress and exhaust us, and yet we find it hard to stop.

"A day of worry is more exhausting than a week of work."
John Lubbock

Worry doesn't 'feel' nice either. It can make your stomach feel tight; you may not want to eat, or even talk to others and, as we mentioned a moment ago, it might stop you sleeping. It all has a nasty habit of growing, so you start off with one worry then it somehow spreads and you find yourself worrying about all sorts of other things. If you have worked through some of the earlier activities on managing your thoughts, then the tips for handling worry shouldn't come as too much of a surprise:

- **Identify what the real central worry is.** If, for example, you are worrying about an interview, what is the real worry? Is it talking to strangers, or perhaps being asked a question you can't answer, or maybe a fear that if it doesn't go well you will be disappointed? It doesn't matter what it is, identifying it will help you tackle it effectively.

- **Try to be rational.** Many worries are either irrational or out of proportion, so try to give your worries a reality check. How likely is it that what you are worrying about happening will happen? Yes, there is always a chance, but being realistic can help to reduce the worry you feel.

- **Share the worry.** Not only might it bring a bit of relief to you, but friends can often be much more realistic and help you to be rational about the worry. They can help to get it all back into proportion sometimes. Even saying it aloud can help us see how silly or inaccurate it might be.

- **Turn it on its head.** So, if you are worried that an interview will be terrible, simply try saying to yourself that it's going to be great. Take it further and tell yourself you'll perform well answering the questions – this is affirming what you want to happen.

- **Allow yourself to visualise the desired outcome.** If you are worried about how something is going to turn out and it hasn't happened yet, then just rewrite the story and make it the one you want. Think back to Chapter 7 on harnessing the subconscious, visualise, add detail and get in touch with the emotion.

"What worries you masters you."
Haddon W. Robinson

One of the biggest drawbacks of worry is that it robs us of our peace in the present. Nearly always worry is about the future and what might happen (although sometimes it can be driven by the past and worrying about the impact of maybe something we have done or said). If there is something practical you can do to lessen your worry that isn't going to be harmful for someone else, then do it.

"Worry does not empty tomorrow of its sorrow; it empties today of its strength."
Corrie ten Boom

If you have been fretting that something you said may have upset someone and you can check with them, then simply apologise or explain that while you may have meant what you said you didn't mean to hurt them, or say whatever else is appropriate.

But if it is about future worries, then that can't really help. Sometimes more information stops our worry and anxiety, so finding out more about what is expected or where we need to go to or what will happen might help. But if it is a worry that is based on something that only *might* happen in the future, then the best way to handle it is to root yourself in the present.

Try distraction, either reading, chatting about something else, or immersing yourself in a task that takes concentration. Another way to immerse yourself in the present is to be mindful or meditate. If it is not something you have done before, then simply try taking a few deep breaths and focusing on your breath, and every time your thoughts stray back to your worry remember that you can choose your thoughts and you can simply go back to focusing on your breath.

Whatever the reason behind your procrastination there is something you can do. You may have heard the expression 'eat your frogs', which may be from a French proverb, although I've also seen it attributed to Mark Twain. The idea is that if you have to do something you don't want to – eating a frog – then the best course of action is to get on and do it. When we do it, almost always, we will find it is not as bad as we thought.

In short, the best way to overcome procrastination is simply to stop procrastinating and start doing!

CHAPTER 15
Overcoming overwhelm

Before we consider overwhelm itself, let's first look at how we use questions as they can be a powerful tool in managing feelings of overwhelm.

Questions are a hugely important part of life. They are one of the tools we use to gather information. They can help us clarify all kind of matters and, of course, find out what people think. Questioning is also one of the tools used by many counsellors and therapists to get to what might be the root of issues and, of course, to reframe information and encourage clients to do the same.

We can also learn to question ourselves to gain clarity on why we feel the way we do, or why we experience some of the worries or anxieties that we do and why some feelings may be overwhelming.

But what questions should we ask and how do we go about it? By now you will know that the subconscious mind is much more powerful than our conscious mind, and self-questioning is one of the ways we can help to unleash its power in helping us to be honest with ourselves and identify what some of the bottom-line issues that we face are, rather than the superficial ones that often fill our minds. Use the following questions to explore any negative feelings that may be bothering you.

What am I afraid of?

Often the issues we face are actually rooted in one sort of fear or another. So, for example, if you find yourself worrying obsessively about the fact that you might have upset someone, then if you ask yourself the question, "What are you really afraid of?" it will usually be that the person in question might reject you or think somehow less of you. This fear in turn is usually rooted in low self-esteem.

What's the worst that can happen?

Another useful question is, "What's the worst that can happen?" This is particularly useful when you are having trouble making a decision – again, asking this question will often take you to the underlying issue. In many cases, though certainly not all, this underlying fear may be a fear of failure. The purpose is, in a sense, to 'expose' this fear so you can begin to deal with it. What is wrong with failure? It is a common experience of life, but often people are afraid that they will let others down or let themselves down in some way. Hopefully, if you had a 'failure mindset', an underlying belief that you were somehow destined to failure and would never be successful, you have been able to deal with it through the work that we did earlier in Chapter 15. As I mentioned earlier, the subconscious is powerful and will work hard to ensure that what we really concentrate on comes to pass.

If I were ---------- what would be different?

This can be a really powerful question to ask yourself and you can make it fit your own circumstances perfectly by inserting whatever your best outcome would be in the blanks.

For example, if you aren't feeling happy, insert that and ask yourself, "If I were happy, what would be different?" Perhaps you would feel more secure with your partner, perhaps you would have a job you enjoy, or be thinner, healthier or whatever. It is a great way to crystallise your thoughts. But more importantly, once again, it can help you to identify the issues that are really causing you to feel the way you do. In the early chapters of the book we considered a lot of the big stuff, big dreams, the big picture of our lives, so by now the feelings may be of anxiety or worry. In that case ask yourself, "If I were to feel calm, what would be different?"

What is my usual response to this?

We humans can develop habits very quickly. Some might be good habits, but of course others may be habits that do us no good at all. When you are in a situation try asking yourself how you usually respond – usually this works best with a situation that is repeated, perhaps feeling angry or getting into unhelpful arguments with people or feeling overwhelmed with what needs to be done.

As humans, we can find ourselves in a situation where it is perfectly reasonable, perhaps even helpful or protective, to act in a particular way, but then we can find ourselves habitually acting in that way even if it has stopped serving any useful purpose for us, or even if it is something that actually causes us harm. For example, people who have grown up without establishing close attachments to significant others, or grown up experiencing significant rejection, will sometimes develop a self-protective relationship sabotage that says reject others before they reject you. But this habitually drawing back or alienating of others can remain a destructive habit into adulthood and the results can be very detrimental to leading a happy fulfilled life.

When you have thought about how you usually react or respond, then you can ask the follow-up question:

Is there a better/more helpful response?

Questions can be useful in identifying what the underlying issues may be that are causing you problems, but of course asking and answering the questions is only the first part; changes in how we behave and respond are also likely to be necessary.

But let us think for a bit about overwhelm, that sense of drowning in either tasks or emotions, or a sense that a feeling is so overpowering it simply buries us.

Whether in business or life, almost everyone will experience overwhelm at times. It could be feeling that there is just too much to do, or that you have too many responsibilities. Alternatively, it might be more of an emotional overwhelm if life has been challenging with maybe illness or break-ups, financial or other worries. Feeling overwhelmed makes everything seem worse and often we can be almost 'paralysed', feeling that we don't know where to start or how to tackle the tasks or feelings, or there can be a tendency to be stressed and rush about like the proverbial headless chicken, being busy but often achieving nothing. But however you respond to overwhelm, these simple steps will help you to manage and get your life and emotions back on track.

Create some space

The first step is to allow yourself a little bit of space. This could be stepping away from your desk, going for a walk or taking half a day for yourself. It's easy to think you haven't the time, but sometimes you just need to do this to get yourself back on track. When we feel overwhelmed it can show itself in different ways; we may feel physically stressed, possibly almost manic with busyness, or we may feel apathetic and that we can't face anything.

Clearing a bit of space is essential to feel the emotion and then perhaps question why we are feeling the way we are. But we also need a determination to face the situation rather than trying to bury your head in the sand, or under the duvet, and sometimes, strangely, we do that by not giving ourselves any space. We have probably seen it in others; in fact, it is easier often to spot in others – they are so over-busy but somehow can't stop. Busyness is a great way to avoid facing emotion or even dealing with some practical problems or issues, but doing that will often store up problems for ourselves later on.

Acknowledge it

Be honest with yourself – it's all too much. It is important to acknowledge the existence of your overwhelm, otherwise you'll end up just literally taking a break then going back to exactly how things were, which will have the same result. Something needs to change. If the overwhelm is the result of a specific situation, a big event for example, then it may all pass when the event passes, but usually overwhelm creeps up gradually because you are too busy for too long. If it is an emotional overwhelm, it's usually because you have been hiding feelings to keep going until they all sort of spill out. In this case, you also need to acknowledge how you feel; you may be strong, but emotions can take their toll, so you need to develop some strategies to take care of yourself like the ones highlighted in Chapter 12.

Assess your priorities

Once you have created some space for yourself then assess your priorities. Sometimes it helps to write everything down – all the things that are making you feel overwhelmed. Then look at the list and identify what the really important things are, not the urgent things but the important things. Different things will be important at different times. Ask yourself what your priorities are right now. There are usually things that are important but which can take a back seat for a while. There are often other things that actually might add to overwhelm every day, like a mountain of emails you haven't opened that somehow worry you. Identifying certain priorities can have an almost immediate positive impact.

"Instead of saying I don't have time, try saying it's not a priority. Changing our language reminds us that how we spend our time is a choice. If we don't like how we are spending an hour, we can choose differently."
Laura Vanderkam

Delegate or get help

Lots of people find it tough to delegate or ask for help for a whole host of reasons. It doesn't matter if it's a business owner who is afraid others won't do things the way they themselves would or someone who feels they must never cut corners with cooking even though they are now studying. Insisting on doing it all yourself is often a sure-fire way to prevent growth. Plus, if you regularly feel overwhelmed, maybe it is simply time to outsource some tasks or ask others to help. If you feel overwhelmed because of family and domestic responsibilities, then sometimes adjustments need to be made. It is okay to ask people to help; we can all find the going hard at times and it really is a better option than letting ourselves become overwhelmed.

Determine to be different

We all know the saying that if we keep doing what we've always done we'll get exactly the same results. If you don't want to find yourself in this position again, then decide to do things differently. Make a plan, set aside some time to relax, and perhaps try to improve your organisation, planning or prioritisation.

If it is emotions that overwhelm you, then there are steps you can take to manage that, and we will look at emotions in the next chapter.

CHAPTER 16
Regulation and resilience

Emotions are what make us human in many ways and are responsible for our happiest moments and our saddest, our times of greatest contentment and our times of greatest anxiety. The emotions, as we saw earlier, are governed by hormones and other chemicals, which in turn may be influenced by a whole host of other factors. But unless we learn ways to regulate our emotions, then they can leave us living a life that can feel a bit like a rollercoaster.

Self-regulation has become a bit of a buzzword in certain circles. What it means is the process by which we regulate ourselves – not rocket science – but going one step further it means how we get ourselves from functioning with our 'primitive' or survival brain, which happens in a protective way when there is a threat for example, to behaving in a calm and measured way, which is usually easier when we feel safe and secure.

"The biggest challenge to self-control is emotional regulation. Successful people know how to make their emotions their servants rather than their masters."
Paul T. P. Wong

Like almost everything in our body and brain things happen for a reason. When we are under threat lots of chemicals are released causing us to respond – usually in a fight or flight way. But in modern society here in the Western world usually there isn't an actual threat but a perceived threat, so we become aroused and emotional and our bodies are flooded with chemicals, even when the 'threat' is not real.

Think about when you are afraid, or extremely angry or sad. With a few exceptions, as adults we usually manage to calm ourselves down, though depending on the level of distress this may take a little while. We also probably all know that there are some people who find this a bit more difficult than others or some occasions when for other reasons we find it harder.

It is thought that self-regulation is essential for health and happiness. It is the mechanism we use to soothe ourselves, calm ourselves and cheer ourselves up. It allows us to not just concentrate on immediate reactions but respond in a more planned way.

"Self-regulation will always be a challenge, but if someone is going to be in charge it might as well be me."
Daniela Akst

It is worth remembering that emotions can't easily be put into neat compartments. We may categorise them as good or bad in terms of how they make us feel, but even that varies. There are times when crying feels wholly negative and other times when we can almost 'enjoy' a good cry. The important thing is accepting that the emotions themselves are neutral; it is our interpretation of them and response to them that may be positive or negative. Emotions are an essential part of our humanity, but sometimes we need to learn how to express them appropriately and manage their impact.

So, how do we manage these emotions we face every day? We know, for example, that feeling stressed constantly every day can cause us physical and mental harm, so it is important that we manage them in a way that helps us live life to the full and enjoy all the positive aspects of being emotional human beings while making sure we are not battered about by every emotion that might surface through the day.

So, what is the right way to manage emotions and how can we do that? Well, it is not helpful to bury them, though there is a difference between that and holding back your tears in response to some news UNTIL you feel in a place where you can express your emotions safely and comfortably, possibly when you are at home or with someone you trust. Simply squashing down all the feelings because they are uncomfortable is a recipe for disaster. The trick is to find ways to express them appropriately.

"Unexpressed emotions will never die. They are buried alive and will come forth later in uglier ways."
Sigmund Freud

Appropriate expression

Emotions do need to be expressed, but as adults who have learned to 'regulate' there are elements of choice about how and when we do that. Feeling anger, for example, is not necessarily a negative thing. It is a reasonable response to feeling hurt or betrayed. However, we have probably all had occasions where we have wisely 'chosen' to respond in a way that is measured.

Our response to emotions is also linked to our general wellbeing. Often if we are tired or overworked, we will respond more negatively, perhaps snapping at others for a slight misdemeanour! Taking care of our physical and mental wellbeing will help.

While it remains true that the impact of some emotions can be negative or positive, emotions in themselves simply exist, and we may experience contrasting emotions at the same time in response to one stimulus, feeling happy for example about a new job but sad that we'll have to leave old friends.

By embracing our emotions and learning to manage them in ways that limit the negative impact we can enjoy the 'colour' of emotions and what they bring to our lives while not suffering the potentially damaging effects that unregulated emotions bring.

Self-regulation doesn't mean we should ignore our emotions – which is hard to do anyway – or never show or acknowledge our emotions. What it means is having good mechanisms to manage them so we can use what they give us, remembering that emotions can be a great motivation to action.

"To be aware of your own emotions and to learn how to self-regulate those is an important part of any kind of management of the intuitive or sensitive nature."
Heidi Sawyer

How do we learn to regulate ourselves?

Like any other skill it is learned. Look at a baby or toddler and you will see that they are not able to self-regulate at all. If they are hungry, tired, cold or want comfort, they let you know. When they are in that state their heart rate is raised, they may be red in the face and there is no doubt at all they are not happy. What then happens, providing there is a caring adult around, is that usually the baby will be picked up, soothed, rocked and given what they need, food or a clean nappy etc.

Gradually when that is repeated hundreds of times neural pathways are formed and it means that over time most people learn to calm themselves, though that process takes years, and it happens only when a 'connected' adult can help them. But this needs to happen repeatedly for babies and small children so the right brain architecture is laid down to enable an adult to regulate their own emotions.

Self-regulation as an adult

Personality plays a part and we will all face some situations where it is harder to regulate ourselves than others, for example we may find something causes a lot of anxiety if alone but if with others, especially people we trust, we may not be so anxious. Our ability to regulate ourselves may also depend on our physical condition. If we are in pain or feeling ill, or even if we are hungry or tired, we may find it harder to regulate ourselves than we would at other times.

But almost every adult who can regulate has developed strategies that help them, and these vary depending on the emotion, but will often involve:

• Pausing for a moment BEFORE reacting to a situation

- Viewing difficult situations as a challenge that can be overcome

- Using specific calming strategies like mindfulness or deep breathing to calm yourself

- Choosing to see the good in others

- Concentrating on what is good and going well not things that aren't

- Spending time with people that are trusted and talking about any problems or about feelings

- Understanding that thoughts and especially fears are not always accurate, e.g. worries about things that are very unlikely to ever happen

- Acknowledging emotions and identifying them before you begin to 'regulate'

"The soul always knows what to do to heal itself; the challenge is to silence the mind."
Caroline Myez

Developing resilience

But in some ways the best way to get better at self-regulation is to practise. By that I mean not waiting for a situation when you must summon the strength to regulate yourself but building into your life and habits things that will help, and it's no surprise these are things that will have a beneficial impact on health and wellbeing in general.

In short, I'm talking about looking after your body and your mind. So, it's back to healthy diets, getting enough exercise, having balance in your life so you aren't always feeling stressed, and doing things that help you like having hobbies, spending time with people that are positive and share your values, and making a determined effort to be grateful and optimistic. But it can also help to develop a regular practice where you still your mind. Learning to be in the present and focus on the here and now will help you be able to put a few minutes space between an event happening and then reacting to it. When you have 'reacted' or when you are feeling stressed then there are a range of other things that will help and, as adults, we have usually worked out things that are effective for us and these might include:

- exercise

- talking

- eating

- listening to music

- watching TV

- cooking

- being creative

- having time alone

Recognise and feel the emotion, learn to express it in a healthy way, calm yourself and then choose your response in a rational and measured way.

We probably all accept that if we want to improve physical strength we need to train our bodies in some way. Building emotional resilience is much the same, learning to be emotionally strong and able to handle the knocks life may bring and our emotional response to those knocks. This involves taking care of ourselves, identifying what and who can help us and practising skills that will build our ability to be emotionally resilient.

Activity 15

For this activity begin by identifying the strategies you currently use to help when you feel particularly emotional and note them down.

Then think of any other things that might help that you haven't tried, and if they seem 'appealing' and possible, then note them down and resolve to try them at some point to build up your repertoire of helping strategies.

It is also worth thinking about people that you may go to if you feel you need support. There's no harm in extending that circle a little by thinking of others that may be able to help you – in some ways you can't have too many supporters.

Spend a few moments identifying things that have caused you to be emotional and focus on a time where you didn't feel you managed the emotion very well.

Think about ways you could have handled it differently and what stopped you doing that. Make a note of the 'lesson learnt'.

The purpose of this is not to be self-critical but to identify even more ways or people that can help you become emotionally robust and more resilient.

CONCLUSION
Make it magnificent now ...

As I said at the very beginning of this book, happiness and success mean very different things to different people. Whatever your idea of happiness or success is, it's okay. As long as it is *your* idea of what would make you feel fulfilled and not that of someone else, or indeed something you think 'ought' to make you feel happy and fulfilled, then that is the life you should seek.

Being happy and fulfilled is what you deserve; being successful on your own terms is what you deserve. Although emotions don't exist one at a time, it is quite usual to feel happy about something but sad or perhaps anxious about something else. Most people will have a sense of whether, on balance, their life is one they love ... or not.

If not, then the reality is you can change it. I know that some situations are more challenging than others, but there are almost always some things that can change.

It is not selfish to create a life you love. The likelihood is you will be kind and grateful and take any responsibilities you have seriously. People who live lives they love often feel they have more to offer to others. When we allow others to manipulate or 'guilt' us into living a life that is not fulfilling, we let ourselves down and we prevent others enjoying the fruits of our happiness, success and fulfilment.

"Life is about change. Sometimes it's painful. Sometimes it's beautiful. But most of the time it is both."
Lana Lang

If you bought this book, then the chances are the time is right for you to make changes, for you to begin to allow yourself to dream and be honest with yourself and others about those dreams and then to set about creating a life you will love – to make it magnificent now. That may mean some emotional upheaval as you start to unpack the unhelpful limiting beliefs or mindsets that might have prevented you living the life you want in the past. It may mean challenges as you start to look at areas of your life that are not as you would wish and seek to change them, but change is an integral part of life.

It bears repeating that some events are life-changing and adapting to the changes from these will take time, and this book is not designed for those who may be experiencing significant emotional issues and may benefit from professional help.

Often the biggest changes that occur are within us, in the way we see things, in the way we might appreciate things we hadn't before. In almost every situation the journey towards a happier, more successful and fulfilling life begins with us.

"The greatest discovery of all time is that a person can change his future by merely changing his attitude."
Oprah Winfrey

... and don't give up!

Of course, the process of change may take time and there are bound to be some low points. So, I'm going to leave you with a few tips for those days when the going seems tough so you can have a quick fix while on your personal journey to creating a life you love. It's a list you can refer back to if and when you need to. Some of these things are a recap of points we've covered earlier in the book, included here for handy future reference.

Do it anyway

So, you don't feel like getting out of bed or going to your office or work – just do it anyway. It's amazing how just getting on with the day can improve your mood. It's often wise to wear something you feel good in, slap on a smile and then just DO IT.

Give yourself a treat

It doesn't have to be big or expensive. You can often get a real lift just from treating yourself to a nice coffee or arranging to meet a mate for lunch – or even taking a few treats into the office. Of course, it doesn't have to be food- or drink-orientated; maybe buy yourself a nice new pen or notebook, anything you fancy that will just give you a bit of an instant lift.

Change your routine

Whatever the reason for your low mood, feeling that things are mundane or routine certainly won't help. So, if it's possible and obviously it isn't always, then schedule something a bit different to fit into your day. Even a job you have been putting off like tidying up an area or filing cabinet can help simply because it's different. And on a day like this it could be just what you need to lift your mood – there is a lot of satisfaction in getting something done that you have been putting off.

Enjoy a bit of nature

There is something very uplifting about nature. If you can make time for a walk outside, in a park for example, it can be a real boost. If that isn't possible, then you can always use the internet – there are lots of clips of sea, rivers, trees, fountains etc. – second best but it can still help to lift your mood.

Plan something for the future

We all enjoy having something to look forward to – remember the high that you get when you book a trip or a nice weekend away with friends or family. It doesn't have to be as big as a holiday, unless your down days are very rare. Organising a trip out, seeing someone you haven't seen for a while, a nice meal out or visit to the cinema can all do the trick of giving you something to look forward to and help you get through a tricky day.

Make a list of things you can be grateful for

It's such an old idea to 'count your blessings', but it does really work, and there is evidence it does change your mood: https://successstory.com/inspiration/why-being-grateful-is-great-for-you

So, get out paper and pen and find something you can be grateful for – guaranteed there will be something – and write it down, and usually once you start you'll be able to think of lots of other things to add.

Do a quick life stocktake

We all have up days and down days, but sometimes our mood is the body's way of telling us something isn't right. Maybe we aren't getting enough sleep, we've let our exercise regime slip or maybe our diet is lacking in a lot of nutrients. But there are other possible causes. An occasional down day is quite normal, but maybe there are some areas of life that we just aren't that happy about. If that is the case, be honest with yourself and decide to make some changes.

Think positive thoughts

It is true that often it's not our situation that causes us problems but our thoughts about that situation. I'm not saying it is easy, but our thoughts are something we can control, or at least something we can LEARN to control. If you find yourself plagued by depressing thoughts, then make a point of actively trying to think positive thoughts.

Determine NOT to beat yourself up

One of the problems with having a bit of a low mood is that for many of us it signals an onset of 'harsh criticism' – FROM OURSELVES. Problem is, clearly it just makes things worse, so decide NOT to do that. A good way of framing it is to think about what you would say to a friend in your position. We are somehow able to be a lot kinder to others than we often are with ourselves.

Indulge in some laughter

It doesn't matter if it's listening to jokes, watching a favourite sitcom or even some crazy cat videos on YouTube – laughter lightens our mood as it releases some feel-good hormones, so even a few snatched minutes on a coffee break can do wonders for your mood.

And finally, to keep yourself motivated while you 'Make It Magnificent' don't forget to join the Facebook group of the same name:

https://www.facebook.com/groups/makeitmagnificent/

You can also follow me on Twitter @sheilattuned or Instagram https://www.instagram.com/sheilamulvenney and visit the website www.attunededucation.com for upcoming live events and workshops in your area.

Wishing you success and happiness on your terms and a life you love to live.

Lightning Source UK Ltd.
Milton Keynes UK
UKHW010145090219
336979UK00005B/545/P